Twayne's New Critical
Introductions to Shakespeare

For
William and Alexander

Twayne's New Critical Introductions to Shakespeare

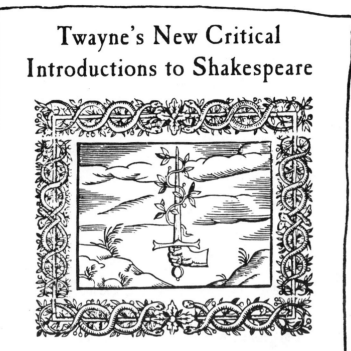

JULIUS CAESAR

Vivian Thomas

University of Birmingham

TWAYNE PUBLISHERS · NEW YORK
An imprint of Macmillan Publishing Co.

Published in the United States by Twayne Publishers,
imprint of Macmillan Publishing Co.,
866 Third Avenue, New York, NY 10022

Published simultaneously in Great Britain by
Harvester Wheatsheaf
Campus 400, Maylands Avenue, Hemel Hempstead, Herts.

Twayne's New Critical Introductions to Shakespeare, no. 13

Library of Congress Cataloging-in-Publication Data

Thomas, Vivian
    Julius Caesar / by Vivian Thomas.
       p. cm. — (Twayne's new critical introductions to Shakespeare
    series : 13)
       Includes bibliographical references (p.   ) and index.
       ISBN 0-8057-8729-1 (cloth). — ISBN 0-8057-8730-5 (paper)
       1. Shakespeare, William, 1564–1616. Julius Caesar. 2. Caesar,
    Julius, in fiction, drama, poetry, etc. 3. Rome in literature.
    I. Title. II. Series: Twayne's new critical introductions to
    Shakespeare : no. 13.
    PR2808.T49   1992
    822.3'3—dc20   92-21951
                                                  CIP

Titles in the Series

GENERAL EDITOR: GRAHAM BRADSHAW

General Editor's Preface

The *New Critical Introductions to Shakespeare* series will include studies of all Shakespeare's plays, together with two volumes on the non-dramatic verse, and is designed to offer a challenge to all students of Shakespeare.

Each volume will be brief enough to read in an evening, but long enough to avoid those constraints which are inevitable in articles and short essays. Each contributor will develop a sustained critical reading of the play in question, which addresses those difficulties and critical disagreements which each play has generated.

Different plays present different problems, different challenges and excitements. In isolating these, each volume will present a preliminary survey of the play's stage history and critical reception. The volumes then provide a more extended discussion of these matters in the main text, and of matters relating to genre, textual problems and the use of source material, or to historical and theoretical issues. But here, rather than setting a row of dragons at the gate, we have assumed that 'background' should figure only as it emerges into a critical foreground; part of the critical endeavour is to establish, and sift, those issues which seem most pressing.

So, for example, when Shakespeare determined that *his* Othello and Desdemona should have no time to live together, or that Cordelia dies while Hermione survives, his deliberate departures from his source material have a critical significance which is often blurred, when discussed in the context of lengthily detailed surveys of 'the sources'. Alternatively, plays like the *The Merchant of Venice* or *Measure for Measure* show Shakespeare welding together different 'stories' from quite different sources, so that their relation to each other becomes a matter for critical debate. And Shakespeare's dramatic practice poses different critical questions when we ask — or if we ask: few do — why particular characters in a poetic drama speak only in verse or only in prose; or when we try to engage with those recent, dauntingly specialised and controversial textual studies which set out to establish the evidence for authorial revisions or joint authorship. We all read *King Lear* and *Macbeth*, but we are not all textual critics; nor are textual critics always able to show where their arguments have critical consequences which concern us all.

Just as we are not all textual critics, we are not all linguists, cultural anthropologists, psychoanalysts or New Historicists. The diversity of contemporary approaches to Shakespeare is unprecedented, enriching, bewildering. One aim of this series is to represent what is illuminating in this diversity. As the hastiest glance through the list of contributors will confirm, the series does not attempt to 'reread' Shakespeare by placing an ideological grid over the text and reporting on whatever shows through. Nor would the series' contributors always agree with each other's arguments, or premisses; but each has been invited to develop a sustained critical argument which will also provide its own critical and historical context — by taking account of those issues which have perplexed or divided audiences, readers, and critics past and present.

Graham Bradshaw

Contents

Preface

Editors of *Julius Caesar* frequently quote the account of a Swiss visitor to London who, writing in September 1599, described an enjoyable visit to a theatre where he saw a performance of the play:

> After lunch on September 21st, at about two o'clock, I and my party crossed the river, and there in the house with the thatched roof we saw an excellent performance of the tragedy of the first Emperor Julius Caesar with about fifteen characters; after the play, according to their custom they did a most elegant and curious dance, two dressed in men's clothes, and two in women's.[1]

This document helps with the dating of the play and provides a rare contemporary account of a performance of one of Shakespeare's plays – if it *was* Shakespeare's *Julius Caesar*, for, like the play itself, Thomas Platter's reference gives rise to an uncertainty which is not amenable to resolution.[2]

Probably written in 1599, *Julius Caesar* is widely recognised as a watershed in Shakespeare's dramatic writing, coming at the mid-point in his career, dividing most of the comedies and histories from the tragedies. As Helen Gardner puts it: 'He was at the height of his powers and his popularity when he turned to the great sequence of tragedies which begins with *Julius Caesar*, and virtually created our modern concept of what tragedy is.'[3] Indeed, it is a play which challenges the very concept of genre. Muriel Bradbrook has referred to *Julius Caesar* as 'the first modern political drama of the English stage'.[4] It has also been described as an example of that most popular of Elizabethan and Jacobean genres, the revenge tragedy.

It seems likely that *Julius Caesar* was chosen to open Shakespeare's Globe Theatre. This deceptively complex play at once achieved a popularity that it has never lost. Certainly, the play offers the modern reader and the theatre-goer the same fresh and exciting challenge that it presented to the first Elizabethan audience – it invites assessments of characters, encourages debates about political judgements and historical events, and analysis of dramatic form. Although the play possesses the surface clarity of polished marble, close scrutiny reveals enigmas which find expression both in critical commentary and in its stage history. Even the specific location of the sunrise is a matter of dispute (II.i) and it is just one of the many issues that are unresolved for the audience. Indeed, Shakespeare's play takes its place in a long history of debate about the relative merits of Julius Caesar and Marcus Brutus and of the circumstances surrounding the events leading up to and stemming from Caesar's assassination on 15 March 44 BC.

Beginning with some preliminary comments on the critical reception of the play and its stage history (which requires special acknowledgement of a debt to John Ripley's *'Julius Caesar' on Stage in England and America 1599–1973*), this book examines relevant textual considerations before evaluating competing generic conceptions of the play and exploring the significance of Shakespeare's creation of a distinctively Roman world. Closely related to this latter issue is Shakespeare's response to Thomas North's translation of Plutarch's remarkable historical work *The Lives of the Noble Grecians and Romans*. Because of its enormous importance it is usual for editors of *Julius Caesar* to outline Shakespeare's response to his source material, and to delineate carefully the relationship between the historical and dramatic characters and events embraced by the play. The approach adopted here, however, differs from standard practice in that discussion of historical characters and events is tightly interwoven with critical analysis of the play. Deeply influenced by the shaping power of their social universe, Shakespeare's characters employ a distinctive language. Anne Barton makes the point that: 'By keeping the enormous memory of Cicero alive in his tragedy, Shakespeare constantly directs his audience's attention towards Rome as the city of orators and rhetoricians: a place where the art of persuasion was cultivated, for better or for worse, to an extent unparalleled in any other society', and adds: 'In *Julius Caesar*, the art of persuasion has come to permeate life so completely that people find themselves using it not only to influence others but to deceive themselves.'[5] Thus the play invites an exploration of the protean nature of language and the relationship between character, language and society – facets of the play that are analysed in the chapter on style.

This discussion of *Julius Caesar* operates within what can be broadly termed the liberal humanist tradition. The last two decades, however, have witnessed the emergence of interpretive methodologies which are in sharp conflict with traditional approaches – though it is important to bear in mind Laurence Lerner's caution that 'there is no such thing as "traditional literary criticism"'. Such terms as 'traditional' or 'mainstream' may provide a useful form of shorthand but they should not be used to obscure 'the enormous variety of critical positions and theories from Plato to Leavis'.[6]

What most, if not all, modernist approaches share is a conviction that the tradition they are attacking is inherently conservative, that its bourgeois ideology not only seeks to preserve existing political structures but is, moreover, critically debilitating rather than vitalising. Yet while there is virtual ideological unity in the charges, in terms of critical techniques there is a paradox: structuralists would seem to denounce liberal humanism for its tendency to go beyond the verbal structure of the text, while new historicists and most other modernists convict liberal humanists of being too tied to the text, of being too introverted. Regarding the former, George Steiner comments:

> Let me try and put very simply what the 'new way' of reading literature which we associate with such awkward words as 'structuralism' or 'semiotics' is fundamentally about. Instead of looking at a poem or passage from a novel in terms of what it says about 'the world out there', in terms of how the words represent or produce external experience, the 'structuralist' critic takes the text to be a complete experience in itself. The action, the only possible truth, is 'inside' the words. We don't ask how they relate to some supposed evidence 'out there', but we look at the manifold ways in which they relate to each other or to comparable verbal structures.[7]

There is no scope here for providing a critique of structuralist and closely related critical approaches (for a tightly reasoned and accessible analysis see Cedric Watts' essay, 'Bottom's children: the fallacies of structuralist, post-structuralist and deconstructionist literary theory'[8]), but some attention must be given to cultural materialism and new historicism, as the adherents of these schools have, in their highly polemical writings, provided a vigorous challenge to liberal humanism. A shared concern of Marxism, cultural materialism, feminism and new historicism is a desire to analyse Shakespeare's plays in more explicitly social and historical contexts.

The main charge against traditional literary criticism is that it takes the text as an artefact, detached from its cultural milieu, and propagates the belief that the text can be analysed and interrogated without reference to any cultural context, past or present. Further, the liberal humanist tradition, it is held, has conspired, overtly or covertly, consciously or subconsciously, to discover in the plays of Shakespeare ideas and perceptions that serve as cultural supports to prevailing socio-political systems. In this way the plays are not merely neutralised by draining off their subversive and potentially destabilising elements, they are co-opted to the service of the state. Thus, the argument runs, conventional criticism has performed a conservative role in packaging Shakespeare for public consumption. The new approaches, in contrast, seek to unpackage the plays by revealing the influence of their cultural origins and displaying tensions and ambivalences arising out of specific historical circumstances. Seen in this way the plays are not timeless artefacts, albeit containing numerous complex structures and verbal patterns, but become demythologised, directly available to historical interrogation. In other words, what has been considered extra-textual, and therefore standing on the periphery of critical discussion, is now seen as intra-textual and essential to any meaningful discussion of the text. Proponents of these new approaches recognise, indeed celebrate, the inevitability of subjectivity and denounce mainstream critics for failing to recognise their own imported and contestable values. In order to convey a genuine perception of the critique of the liberal humanist tradition and the nature of the drive that lies behind the new approaches, it is necessary to examine closely the precise formulations of some of these critics and to provide a feeling of their oppositional tone.

Dollimore and Sinfield, two of the most forthright advocates of cultural materialism, comment:

> cultural materialism does not pretend to political neutrality. . . . Cultural materialism does not, like much established literary criticism, attempt to mystify its perspective as the natural, obvious or right interpretation of an allegedly given textual fact. On the contrary, it registers its commitment to the transformation of a social order which exploits people on grounds of race, gender and class.

The 'old historicists', they rightly claim, provided a misleading picture of the Elizabethan world:

Those of Tillyard's persuasion saw [the metaphysic of order in the Elizabethan period] as consolidating, that is socially cohesive in the positive sense of transcending sectional interests and articulating a genuinely shared culture and cosmology, characterised by harmony, stability and unity. In contrast, materialist criticism is likely to consider the ideological dimension of consolidation – the way, for example, that this world picture reinforces particular class and gender interests by presenting the existing social order as natural and God-given (and therefore immutable).

For these critics rigorous interrogation of social and cultural conditions generates new critical perspectives so that Shakespeare's plays are seen in a fresh light. This is important because: 'Shakespeare's plays constitute an influential medium through which certain ways of thinking about the world may be promoted and others impeded, they are a site of cultural struggle and change.' Or as they put it elsewhere: 'Shakespeare is one of the places where ideology is made.'[9]

And here we draw close to both the historical and political perspectives of these new approaches to Shakespearian criticism. As the editors of a recent book of essays, *Shakespeare Reproduced: The Text in History and Ideology*, express the matter:

Claims about Shakespeare as the bearer of universal truths serve an oppressive function when they render illegitimate readings produced outside the dominant ideologies which secure a society's understanding of what the true is. . . . This volume aims to question claims of Shakespeare's universality and to reveal ways in which historically specific factors determine the 'Shakespeare' produced in criticism, in the classroom, and on the stage.

Having provided a broad general assault on the ideological and critically limiting consequences of according Shakespeare the privileged status of a cultural icon, they go on to make some highly specific objections to mainstream criticism:

Accompanying the contention that Shakespeare depicts a universal and unchanging human nature are often two further claims: first, that the meaning of a Shakespearean text is ineluctably *in* that text (and consequently never changes); and second, that the Shakespearean text resides in an aesthetic zone above ideology. One stark link among these claims is their avoidance of history.[10]

Deeply embedded in new historicism is the feeling that for the most part both Shakespeare's plays and those of his contemporaries, though potentially subversive, operated as a conservative force both in the theatre of Elizabethan and Jacobean England and subsequently. Walter Cohen, for example, points out that:

> Though new historicists know that the theatre was at times subversive, and though they argue that it was inherently ambivalent, their readings of individual Shakespearean plays almost always demonstrate the triumph of containment.... As Tennenhouse argues in *Power on Display*, drama was a 'vehicle for disseminating court ideology'.[11]

James H. Kavanagh has emphasised the peculiar position of Shakespeare and his fellow playwrights and the nature of the pressures exerted upon them. Beginning by citing Kernan's pertinent observation that 'the English Renaissance dramatists, Shakespeare included, were the first writers to work in the marketplace', he goes on to argue:

> As a new kind of ideological entrepreneur still working within traditional patronage relations of literary production, Shakespeare had to keep favour with his court patron – in this case the powerful Lord Chamberlain – who afforded the company political protection, and, literally, licence to work; at the same time, he had to hold the interest of a broad public drawn from London's mercantile, artisanal and working classes.[12]

Perhaps the most striking feature of Shakespeare's society was its rapidly evolving condition: it retained significant elements of feudalism but, simultaneously, displayed many characteristics of the modern world. Above all it witnessed the birth of capitalism. Strangely, the most thorough exploration of the economic life of the period has been undertaken not by the new historicists but by L. C. Knights in *Drama and Society in the Age of Jonson*, written as long ago as 1937. Knights' aim was not simply to show how economic change exerted an influence on the drama, but, more importantly, to reveal how the plays could be used as social documents. Though Knights' findings were rather unexciting and unsurprising, his description of the economic landscape went well beyond anything previously attempted and has yet to be surpassed by any scholar in the field of literary studies. Among other things he reminded students of Elizabethan and Jacobean drama that the period was striking in terms of economic development. The expansion of domestic and foreign trade was accompanied by rapid capital accumulation and a high rate of inflation. And in one respect this was a moment almost unique in British economic history. Knights astutely cited the words of J. M. Keynes, the greatest economist of the twentieth century:

> The greater part of the fruits of the economic progress and capital accumulation of the Elizabethan and Jacobean age accrued to the profiteer rather than to the wage-earner. . . . Never in the annals of the modern world has there existed so prolonged and so rich an opportunity for the business man, the speculator and the profiteer. In these golden years modern capitalism was born.[13]

The dramatist who reflects most fully this phenomenon is, of course, Jonson, for whom the essential quality of economic and social life of the period could be summed up by the phrase 'the acquisitive society'.

Just as L. C. Knights delineated the economic landscape before the arrival of the new historicists, so too did J. W. Lever (in 1971) place great emphasis on the connections between the plays and the social and political realities of the period:

> On the Jacobean stage contemporary issues constantly lurk below the surface of historical or fictitious settings. . . . Chapman explicitly drew attention to the parallels between his protagonist Byron and the Earl of Essex, executed for treason in 1601. Less direct, but un-mistakable in their tenor, are the recurrent allusions to royal favourites, scheming politicians, sycophants, and the network of informers and secret agents through which the contemporary state controlled the lives of its nationals. . . .
>
> Beyond these immediate issues, the serious playwrights of the age were aware of a wider transformation of society taking place throughout Europe and undermining all traditional human relationships. . . . 'The commonwealth', wrote Montaigne, 'requireth some to betray, some to lie, and some to massacre.'. . .
>
> The so-called 'chain of being' was in an advanced condition of rust by the end of the sixteenth century.[14]

Thus new historicists undoubtedly have their precursors. The reciprocal connections between Elizabethan and Jacobean plays and the societies within which they emerged have been widely recognised in the past. What is new in the more recent approaches is a powerful insistence on searching out all possible connections between the diverse elements within the culture and a determination to view society from the bottom up rather than from the top down. As Walter Cohen makes the point:

The deconstructive impact on new historicism is most evident in the constitution of a discursive field that overrides conventional disciplinary or textual demarcations. New historicists are likely to seize upon something out of the way, obscure, even bizarre: dreams, popular or aristocratic festivals, denunciations of witchcraft, sexual treatises, diaries and autobiographies, descriptions of clothing, reports on disease, birth and death records, accounts of insanity.

This approach can be highly invigorating but the danger is that the texts come to be seen as having little interest in themselves except where there is some exciting contextualising material available to illuminate them. The urgent need to range widely beyond the text has been given clear expression by a variety of feminists, many of whom emphasise the limitations of Shakespeare and insist on regarding him as merely a product of his culture. However, as Walter Cohen has commented in criticising a number of British feminists, 'they repeatedly interpret passages from Shakespeare out of context, paying scant attention to the formal qualities of the texts. A social contextualization here leads to an aesthetic decontextualization.'[15]
Anne Barton has also given voice to this anxiety in a review of Greenblatt's recently published book of essays:

> Greenblatt's fondness for dealing with literary texts selectively, detaching a single passage and making it speak for the whole, is another somewhat disquieting characteristic. Works of art have internal as well as external 'resonances'. Their parts respond to one another, are conditioned by their immediate as well as by their social and historical surroundings, in ways he is willing to ignore. . . .
> Greenblatt studiously accumulates so much material from the researches of various social and religious historians, psychologists, political scientists, and anthropologists, that the great works of literature which he continues to address – by Shakespeare, Sidney, Spenser, and other members of what is, on the whole, a very traditional canon – are nearly lost to sight. Quoted from so glancingly as to become almost redundant, they seem less interesting than the material in which he enmeshes them, and sometimes only tenuously related to it. . . .
> *Learning to Curse* is . . . an assemblage of disparate and fragmentary things, arbitrarily juxtaposed, their asserted cultural interconnections all too often depending on Greenblatt's skill at arrangement.[16]

The most recent theoretical schools not only run the risk of 'aesthetic decontextualization', they are also susceptible to other serious criticisms.

In a recent critique of new historicism Richard Levin has exposed a number of conceptual weaknesses. Space does not allow for a thorough examination of Levin's rejection of the 'five discoveries' of new historicism, but two of them – the issue of selfhood and character, and the question of the nature of dramatic illusion – are so germane to the whole critical approach of this essay that they must be examined. Regarding the matter of selfhood and character, Levin comments:

Many of these critics maintain that the modern conception of the self or individual did not yet exist in the Renaissance, or was only coming into existence then. Jonathan Goldberg tells us, without offering any evidence, that to comprehend Shakespeare we must 'give up . . . notions of character as self-same, owned, capable of autonomy and change', because the worldview of his day 'excludes' these 'conceptual categories'. Stephen Greenblatt bases his claim primarily on the trial of an imposter in France in 1559–60, which is supposed to show that the 'conclusions' comprising our sense of identity – that it is an 'inalienable possession', that it is 'primal', 'irreducible', and 'continuous', that it is 'permanently anchored' in our 'biological individuality' – were not 'drawn either explicitly or implicitly by anyone in the sixteenth century. They are irrelevant to the point of being unthinkable'. . . .
Much of the evidence derived from the drama to support the claim that Elizabethans had a radically different concept of the self rests on . . . the belief that inconsistency in characterization cannot be explained by the inadequacies of the playwright or of the state of the art at that time. But a more fundamental error is involved here as well, because the arguments of many of these critics assume that there must be a simple equation between the way characters were represented and the way members of the audience thought of themselves. This is clearly not true. People watching a morality play did not think they were abstractions or personifications. . . . There obviously have been major changes in the representation of character in the drama and in other literary forms from the Middle Ages to the present (and some of these critics have acute observations to make about this), but we have no reason to believe that these corresponded to any changes in the basic conception of selfhood. . . .
I think we would also have to say that the Renaissance conception of selfhood discovered by these critics simply does not make sense. . . .
If anyone still requires specific historical evidence to support this conclusion, we can point to the history books themselves, along with the biographies or 'Lives', that were written during the Renaissance, since

these all necessarily assume that their human 'subjects' possessed selves that were autonomous and united and persisted through time and change. Without those assumptions there could be no history.

It is worth adding here that Shakespeare continually raises the question of what precisely character is and seems particularly interested in the way character is anchored in the community and is shaped by it. Indeed, character torn from its natural ambience does seem to suffer from anomie or alienation, something most powerfully suggested through Calchas in *Troilus and Cressida* (iii.iii.1–12). Moreover, the intimate connection between man and society is revealed in the Roman plays where the shaping power of culture is felt more strongly than anywhere else in Elizabethan and Jacobean drama. Thus, far from possessing a different or more limited conception of character from that prevailing today, Shakespeare in this important respect seems very much our contemporary.

Turning to the important matter of the nature of theatrical illusion, Levin constructs his case as follows:

A number of these critics claim that Elizabethan audiences, unlike those of later times, did not enter into the illusion of a theatrical performance and therefore did not become emotionally involved in it. Graham Holderness explains that 'the Elizabethan theatre was [not] a theatre of illusion', which he associates with 'nineteenth-century theatre', but 'a theatre of alienation', where 'the audience would always sustain an awareness of the constructed artifice of the proceedings, would never be seduced into the oblivion of empathetic illusion'. Derek Longhurst implies the same thing when he says that a modern production of Shakespeare's plays 'misconceives' them, since the 'naturalism' of 'the bourgeois theatre . . . directs an audience towards an empathetic response to individual characters'. . . . Francis Barker contrasts 'bourgeois naturalism' to the 'anti-naturalist' Jacobean theatre, where 'the audience was never captivated by the illusion because the spectacle never produced itself as other than it was'. . . . The evidence for these claims centres on what are held to be the antimimetic or anti-illusionist aspects of the Elizabethan theatre (the absence of scenery, the use of boy actors for female parts, doubling, asides, and so on) and of the play-texts themselves, including inconsistencies in characterization, conflicting perspectives or moral standards, and shifts in rhetorical or poetic style. . . .

If we turn from these theoretical considerations to the actual responses of the people of the Renaissance to their drama – which these critics never mention – we find no evidence of anything resembling the 'distancing' or 'alienation' that was supposed to be so pervasive. On the contrary, these responses all indicate that the plays of this period were expected to create the illusion of 'real' human actions and thus to secure the emotional involvement of the audience, and that they (and their authors) were praised when they succeeded in doing this. . . . Actors of this period were similarly praised for creating the illusion of reality and thereby engaging the spectators' emotions. . . . The same thing applies to the boy actors playing women's parts. . . . I think we could sum up all this evidence by saying that it proves precisely what the new historical critics denied – that viewers and readers of the Renaissance drama were 'captivated by the illusion' and could 'wholly forget themselves' by 'submitting' to it and were 'seduced into the oblivion of empathetic illusion', and therefore that this could not have been a nonidea-of-the-time.[17]

Associated with this issue is the assumed superiority of non-illusionist over illusionist theatre. Catherine Belsey, for instance, has argued that self-reflexive elements in plays underline their fictionality. Watts has provided a strong rebuttal of this claim using Belsey's examples to support his case. Referring to this as: 'The fallacy of the self-referential text', he points to Johnson's comment that: 'Imitations produce pain or pleasure, not because they are mistaken for realities, but because they bring realities to mind.'[18] The numerous self-reflexive moments in Shakespeare's plays are fascinating (none more so than Cassius' and Brutus' comments over the dead body of Caesar III.i.111–18) and operate in a variety of ways, but it is not simply a matter of breaking the dramatic illusion to call attention to the play's fictionality. This view implies an astonishing naïvety on the part of the audience: they either experience total emotional involvement with an abatement of critical faculties, or emotional detachment and a vitalisation of critical faculties. Surely the process is much more complex than this?

What should be immediately apparent from the agenda set forth by distinguished representatives of cultural materialism and new historicism and the critique of Levin is that, far from overthrowing or even marginalising mainstream criticism, these new critical schools have as yet made only a modest contribution to a critical appreciation of the plays *viewed in their widest possible context*. Nevertheless, these new approaches have reinvigorated critical discussion. A good example of recent historicist criticism applied to *Julius Caesar* was provided by John Drakakis in a paper delivered at the International Shakespeare Conference in the summer of 1990 (recently published in *Shakespeare Survey*, vol. 44). One key aspect of his perceptive analysis is drawn on in Chapter 4, but it is worth noting here his emphasis on the implications of the peculiar position occupied by the Elizabethan theatres and the response of theatre companies to these special circumstances:

> when we consider the timing of performances, the constraints of official censorship, the social heterogeneity and consequent volatility of public theatre audiences, along with the desire for respectability amongst practitioners, and the attempts to secure influential patronage, it becomes clear that the liminal status of a theatre such as The Globe effectively guaranteed its relative 'openness' to the production of contradictory cultural meanings. . . .
> Cast in a subversive role, confronted with the demands of official censorship, but nevertheless seeking legitimation, the actual choice of dramatic material would have been crucial. In *Julius Caesar* the Chamberlain's Men could displace their own professional anxieties onto a narrative which, by virtue of its very ambivalence, offered a space for the exploration of the ideology which governs the exchange of representations which take place between society and theatre, centre and margins.

In a play that resonates with uncertainties, the audience is drawn to make judgements from a privileged position, possessing a broader vision than any of the participants. But in making such judgements members of the audience move from a passive position to an active one because they have to confront the issues of power, authority, control, manipulation and sub-ordination. They are intellectually engaged not just with Rome but with their own society. As Drakakis points out:

> There is very little in the play as a whole that does not generate alternative readings, whether it be public display, ritual sacrifice, or psychic phenomena, and it is this hermeneutic instability, the consequence of the existence of two radically opposed forms of authority in Rome, that returns the analysis of motive and action to the space occupied by the theatre which can now claim both to produce *and* to interrogate ideologies.[19]

Julius Caesar abounds in references to acting and theatre, and probes the relationship between character and performance (Casca's description of Julius Caesar's refusal of the crown is only the most striking example of this phenomenon). Marullus and Flavius object to Caesar's images being decked with trophies, the subversion of social ritual by political manipulators, but the bloodied robe of the dead Caesar becomes an even more potent political symbol in Antony's hands, while Rome itself, its very essence, becomes transmuted into the blood of Caesar, which now takes on a sacred quality. Just as characters try to fashion other characters (for example, Cassius' political seduction of Brutus), so too do characters fashion themselves in order to respond to particular needs; for instance, Brutus, in his orchard soliloquy, fashions Caesar into an embryonic tyrant in order to achieve that lofty title of 'soul of Rome'. The ultimate audience for these players is history – future generations who will analyse and assess their motives and achievements. As supporters and opponents of Caesar provide contradictory critiques of the great man, so too the play holds in suspense contrasting evaluations. Both Shakespeare's audience and a modern audience look backwards through the theatrical representation of a major historical event but also look around them observing contemporary events in the light of this dramatic/historical experience. The theatrical performance has the unique quality of being both past and present – acted, in Cassius' words, 'In states unborn, and accents yet unknown!' (iii.i.113). The political implications, therefore, are not dead – they are as alive as the theatrical event itself. As political life is portrayed as intrinsically theatrical, so theatre is intrinsically political. Each critique brings forth a countercritique. And this is true also of literary criticism. Not only do interpretations differ, collide and inter-react, but judgements about the function and nature of such criticism diverge.

Two important points of tangency between new historicism and mainstream criticism relate to the history of the play in performance and Shakespeare's shaping of a highly specific social universe. Even a cursory examination of the play's theatrical history reveals its chameleon-like quality. The rise of fascism, for example, left an indelible mark on productions of the play, something to which the section on stage history draws attention. Secondly, the way in which character is influenced by the prevailing values of society is subject to searching examination by the dramatist. In his creation of Roman worlds Shakespeare could have settled for providing merely background or colour to his drama, but he strove very deliberately for something much more potent. Surprisingly, new historicists have not engaged in a serious analysis of this highly significant process. *Julius Caesar* is a play which encourages recognition of the tensions which animate every society, including the efforts of political élites to represent their actions as motivated by a desire to serve the public good. Despite the differences in overall perspective and in important matters of detail already mentioned, the gap between modernist and mainstream criticism may not be quite as wide as much polemical writing suggests, but this text focuses directly on Shakespeare's created social world rather than attempting to analyse the play as a response to the dramatist's socio-political environment. For students wishing to explore closely new historicist and related modernist approaches some guidance is provided in the Select Bibliography. Obviously there are a number of good individual studies of the play but many of the best essays are contained in works dealing with the Roman plays as a group. The Select Bibliography endeavours to provide a careful selection of the most rewarding of the varied critical studies, and to suggest useful modern studies of the great historical personages who appear in the play or who, like Pompey, haunt it.

Acknowledgements

Quotations from *Julius Caesar* are from the Arden edition edited by T. S. Dorsch (Methuen, London and New York 1955).

I owe a debt of gratitude to Graham Bradshaw for his many helpful suggestions and constant encouragement during the writing of this book and to Jackie Jones and her associates at Harvester Wheatsheaf for their valuable assistance. Ivy Scott kindly read the manuscript and cast a practised eye over my syntax. Special thanks are due to my wife who typed and corrected the manuscript through its various stages.

The Stage History

Ben Jonson's numerous allusions to the play suggest that it was frequently staged during the first few decades of the seventeenth century. Antony's lines:

> O judgement, thou art fled to brutish beasts,
> And men have lost their reason.
>
> (iii.ii.106–7)

are parodied in *Every Man Out Of His Humour* with Clove's comments to Orange: 'Then comming to the pretty *Animal*, as reason long since is fled to *Animals* you know.' The same lines are echoed in *The Wisdome of Doctor Dodypoll* (Stationers' Register 1600) when Alberdure leaves the stage, crying: 'Then reason's fled to animals I see,/ And Ile vanish like Tobacco smoke.' Leonard Digges, also, gives a clear indication that the play was popular on the Jacobean stage. In his prefatory verses to the First Folio he singles out the quarrel scene for special commendation, and this praise is elaborated in an extended or revised version of his epistle intended for the 1632 Second Folio, but eventually prefixed to the 1640 edition of Shakespeare's poems.

There are few detailed accounts of seventeenth-century productions before 1660, though there are references to 'Caesar's Tragedy' in the Whitehall season of 1611–12, and to court performances in January 1637 and November 1638. After the Restoration considerable distinction was achieved by Charles Hart as Brutus, Michael Mohun as Cassius and Edward Kynaston as Antony. The play was appreciated primarily for its vigour and the force of its central characters. 'Thomas Betterton, the greatest actor of the late seventeenth century, played Brutus as a majestic philosophical stoic', symbolising the struggle for republican freedom against the iniquity of autocratic rule. This interpretation, together with its concomitant political vision, was to last to the middle of the eighteenth century. An indication of the play's popularity can be gauged by the fact that between 'Betterton's last Brutus in 1708 and James Quin's last in 1751 only five seasons passed without a performance'.[1] The play was usually cut in the eighteenth century (in contrast to the seventeenth) with the aim of accentuating Roman dignity and reducing its anachronisms and ambivalences. The proscription scene was generally omitted. Psychological ambiguities, scenic presentation and the influence of the crowd were minimised. After 1751 there were few productions to the end of the century, though the play became popular with the reading public in America.

Philip Kemble's productions which commenced on 29 February 1812 at Covent Garden 'marked a triumphant restoration of *Julius Caesar* to popular favour'.[2] They revelled in classical costume and scenic splendour:

> Roman grandeur was to be realized not only, as hitherto, by fine elocution in strong acting roles, and by classical costumes posed against scene paintings populated by unobtrusive extras, but by the high art of scenic design before which the actors were grouped according to Reynolds's classical principles, while an impressive crowd of supporters reflected Rome's pomp and circumstance.

Although cutting and altering the text even more severely than his eighteenth-century predecessors, Philip Kemble, as Brutus, preserved the notion of the ideal republican, though Charles Kemble elevated the character of Antony, portraying him as the noble avenger of his friend. Perhaps the greatest revelation was Charles Mayne Young's portrayal of Cassius as 'intellectual, thrusting, and high-strung, with a fine range of delivery', achieving 'intense vitality' in sharp contrast to Kemble's 'deliberateness'.[3]

The success of Kemble's productions generated a renewed enthusiasm for the play which lasted for almost half a century (1819 to 1865). The great

names were Charles Mayne Young, William Charles Macready and Samuel
Phelps. Two striking features of Macready's revivals at Covent Garden in
1838–9 and at Drury Lane in 1843 were the 'handsome and scholarly
settings and the populous crowd scenes'. Innovatively, the play was 'directed vigorously to set his protagonists in the context of a living society;
Rome became a city not merely of patricians but of a populace involved in
the actions of the great, a development which pointed towards the modern
populist sense of history', so that '*Julius Caesar*'s Rome was turning from
a far-off classical scene to a mirror of social reality'.[4] Macready presented
the assassination scene with much greater realism than hitherto and also
endeavoured to give a naturalistic response to it. Samuel Phelps' remarkable Cassius testified to the accuracy of Macready's view that he was
'among Shakespeare's most perfect specimens of idiosyncrasy'.[5] As Ripley
comments:

> However adept Phelps was at portraying roughness and irritability, he
> was still more successful in expressing tenderness and rugged pathos;
> and this gift brought a new dimension to Cassius, a quality of softness
> which stood out in dynamic contrast to his habitual asperity.[6]

Phelps, having gained five years' experience playing Cassius to Macready's
Brutus, played the latter part for two decades. Described as 'the last great
English Brutus of the nineteenth century',[7] he favoured sparer sets and
laid less emphasis than Macready on the pre-eminence of Brutus. The
popularity of *Julius Caesar* continued right up to Phelps' last performance at
Drury Lane in 1865. Thereafter productions of the play declined (though
not in the United States) until it received a spectacular revival by Beerbohm
Tree in 1898.

 A watershed in the theatrical history of the play occurred in 1861 with
the visit to London of the Meiningen Court Company. Although dedicated
to ensemble playing, the company engaged a star-actor, Ludwig Barnay,
whose mesmerising Antony became a dominant presence in the play.
Gaining complete control over the dynamically unstable crowd, he made
the Forum scene the climax. All that followed was anti-climax. The Saxe-
Meiningen productions exerted a powerful influence on Beerbohm Tree.
With a first run of over a hundred performances, his productions were
described as opening 'a new epoch in the history of Shakespeare on the
London stage'.[8] In particular, Tree was convinced that Antony was the
dominant character in the play and the Forum scene its highpoint. In order
to speed up the last part of the play and to remove anything which tarnished
Antony's image he cut the text (by 25 per cent). Tree, a remarkably

successful Antony, realised his finest moments in the Forum scene and, with a fine actor, Charles Fulton, playing Caesar, the shift in the balance of the play was reinforced. Perhaps the best clue to Tree's overall vision is to be found in a programme note: 'it is not the historic band of conspirators that strikes the key note of the play. It is not even the mighty figure of Caesar treacherously brought low. It is the feverish pulsing life of the imperial city.'[9] This perception was not lost on reviewers: the *Telegraph*, for example, drew attention to the fact that 'the scenery, costume and colouring made it a replica not of the last days of the Republic but of the hey-day of the Empire' and commended Tree's theatrical instinct: 'to make his Rome superbly, theatrically itself, he had to give back to his audience their idea of Rome made bigger and better and three-dimensional'.[10] Thus the Saxe-Meiningen production and that of Beerbohm Tree created a shift in the balance of the play: Antony became the central figure. Likewise Rome itself took on new life with its magnificent scenic splendour and its vibrant plebeians.

With literally thousands of performances, the popularity of *Julius Caesar* in the United States reached its peak between 1871 and 1891. The two most notable productions were those of Edwin Booth at Booth's Theater which ran for 85 nights from December 1871, and Jarratt and Palmer's which opened at the same New York theatre exactly five years later and achieved a record run of 103 performances. American productions during the last decade of the nineteenth century and the first third of the twentieth seem to have been undistinguished. The impact of Orson Welles' New York production of 1937, however, was as immediate as it was powerful. Subtitled *Death of a Dictator*, it ran for an unprecedented 157 performances. So severely cut and refashioned that it might best be referred to as an adaptation of Shakespeare's *Julius Caesar*, it caused a sensation. More strikingly than any other production, it reflected the historical circumstances in which it was born. A sense of the theatrical power and social significance of this production is revealed by a few comments from Ripley's summary:

Unlike the solid sets and well-defined movement and business of traditional revivals, this *Caesar* was an elusive, almost symphonic creation of light, shadow, sound, and shifting images caught in a timeless space. Much was suggested, almost nothing represented. Atmosphere was everything.

The production opens with the stage in darkness, and Blitzstein's overture throbbing ominously. A voice suddenly and piercingly cries,

'Caesar', and the lights come up on the arrogantly self-controlled Dictator, in the military dress affected by Mussolini and Hitler, surrounded by subordinates in dark-green uniforms. Civilians in contemporary street clothes look on admiringly. Up-angled shafts of light marked this Caesar well – his striding height, jutting chin, cross-belted military tunic, sleek modern breeches. . . . From the murky abyss beyond the shaft of light in which Caesar stands comes the warning, 'Beware the Ides of March'; but the mysterious speaker disregards orders to 'Come from the throng' and 'Look upon Caesar'. On 'He is a dreamer', the group moves off with shouts of 'Hail, Caesar' and Fascist salutes. . . . This scene with its hard-edged lighting, sinister shadows, staccato 'Hails', and open-palm salutes powerfully evokes the authoritarian mood which permeates the first half of the play. . . .

The Cinna the Poet scene, perhaps the most celebrated feature of the production, caught the imagination of audiences by its unfamiliarity and sheer theatricality. . . .

It is doubtful if this scene has ever been better staged. . . .

The controversial Brutus of Welles was the undisputed pivot of the action. . . .[11]

Clearly this remarkable and seminal production stands out as one of the landmarks in the staging of *Julius Caesar*.

Except for the period of 'black-out' during the Second World War, *Julius Caesar* retained a position of prominence in England for the first half of the twentieth century. During this time there was a gradual reaction against magnificent scenery and the great oratorical mode to a modernism in sets, costumes and acting styles. Memorable productions of the early twentieth century would have to include those of Frank Benson (1890–1933), the famous actor-manager, who cut the text severely to achieve pace at the expense of variety. His portrayal of Antony was acclaimed but he was seldom accompanied by a Brutus or Cassius of equal calibre. Murray Carrington, playing Caesar, conveyed both a greatness and the frailty of a man in decline, and so: 'After at least two centuries of being a figurehead, Caesar at last begins to receive some consideration as a man.' Benson was succeeded by William Bridges-Adams as Festival Director at Stratford-upon-Avon. It was there in August 1919 that he staged 'the first full-text production at a major theatre since the Restoration'. This production 'saw *Caesar* shaped for the first time by the craft of the director rather than the whim of the actor-manager, an innovation crucial to the course of the play in this century'. Thus 'after two centuries of service as a star-vehicle, the play at last assumed an identity of its own'.[12] Bridges-Adams' intention was to achieve an ensemble acting style and, with the use of a fuller text, to obtain an effective structural balance. The inclusion of the proscription scene inevitably showed Antony in a new and less flattering light, but the Forum scene once more attained the stature of the Benson–Tree productions and so the last two acts were anti-climactic.

Robert Atkins' Old Vic production of 1921 was characterised by 'visual starkness', swift, intelligent delivery and the fullest text 'played in London since the Restoration'.[13] One of the advantages of this changing style was later exemplified by Gielgud's Antony in Harcourt Williams' 1930 production at the Old Vic. The presentation of the Forum scene was particularly telling. Standing at the top of a flight of steps with the body of Caesar at his feet 'Gielgud's very first line, spoken as a "natural and hurried appeal for listeners in a tumult", firmly identified the speech as a genuine and natural public event rather than a stock splendour of the stage.'[14] Yet set against this gain was a loss of tragic grandeur. No longer, however, could the part of Caesar be reduced to insignificance: in the Old Vic production of 1935, directed by Henry Cass, Cyril Trouncer was praised for providing 'a study in cold splendour, an inhuman, alarming figure with "a mouth as ruthless as the maw of a shark". . . . Both "the flash of greatness as well as the weakening assault of falling sickness" were clearly etched.' Here, unusually, was a Caesar both formidable *and* vulnerable. Even greater acclaim was lavished on Ion Swinley's Mark Antony: 'Swilling wine with Octavius in the Proscription scene . . . the part was never distorted to pander to naturalistic tastes. While Antony's psychology and behaviour were contemporary and credible, his delivery remained poetic and passionate.'[15] Here was an astute sense of balance between naturalism and the requirements of rhetorical technique.

The failures of modernism were at least as striking as its successes. Henry Cass' 1939 production which opened at the Embassy Theatre 'relied upon contemporary costumes, novel business, and colloquial speaking to point his anti-Fascist moral', but gimmickry proved a great distraction. During the battle scenes, for instance, 'Theatre-goers were less conscious of Brutus' words than of the upturned sugar boxes which furnished his dugout, or the figures in steel helmets with fixed bayonets who crouched distractingly beyond.'[16] This did not prevent Donald Wolfit attempting a modern production at the King's Theatre, Hammersmith, in 1949. Its lack of coherence in terms of costume and style produced a general feeling of bewilderment. Here was a production which left Rome far behind without having any contemporary resonance. If nothing else it demonstrated the danger of being vague about the location in time and place of a play which is highly specific about both.

Diversity has characterised productions on both sides of the Atlantic since 1950. With the advent of what became loosely termed 'Director's theatre', the director became interpreter of the text and, with the collaboration of a designer, expressed his perception of the play in visual and thematic terms. Some of the most acclaimed productions, however, achieved their distinction through the performances of great actors. For instance, the production directed by Anthony Quayle and Michael Langham at the Shakespeare Memorial Theatre in 1950 contained a riveting performance by John Gielgud as Cassius:

> No longer merely a passionate foil to Brutus' tranquillity, Gielgud's lean and hungry Roman emerged as the coiled spring which vitalizes the tragedy.

> In the early scenes he appeared as a fanatical crusader against totalitarianism, burningly sincere, and driven by a torrent of energy. . . . Cassius' political concern was not, in Gielgud's opinion, entirely disinterested, however; at the core of the man and pulsing with deadly vitality was 'an innate sense of frustrated power. . . .'

> His farewells and his death were profoundly noble; and for once Brutus' valediction seemed well-earned.[17]

Another vital aspect of the play was illuminated in Michael Langham's production at Stratford, Ontario, in 1955. He emphasised the play's chronicle quality so that 'the ebb and flow of historic events transcended the men who made them'. Neither the assassination scene nor the Forum scene represented a decisive peak. Momentum was maintained throughout the latter part of the play. 'As an exercise in unfettered action and visual excellence, Langham's *Caesar* could hardly be bettered.'[18] Perhaps the outstanding production of the post-war period was that of Glen Byam Shaw at the Shakespeare Memorial Theatre in 1957:

> Shaw placed Caesar firmly at the play's centre. The action was divided into two major movements: the conspiracy leading to Caesar's death, with the physical presence of the Dictator as the dominant motif; and the fate of the leaderless state after the assassination, with Caesar's spirit, symbolized by a blazing star, never far away.[19]

This Julius Caesar, played by Cyril Luckham, dominated the action in a production which achieved harmony between architecture and acting, as Roy Walker's comments indicate:

> the magnificence of the gold-embroidered crimson toga and the majesty of Cyril Luckham's bearing made him the incarnation of an immutable and pivotal principle of order. This ordered Rome was visible in the massive fluted monoliths of light grey stone, ranged outwards from Caesar as their personal centre in two symmetrical lines. . . . Here was the wide perspective of Caesar's Rome with Caesar himself as the keystone.[20]

Antony's cry of 'Here was a Caesar! When comes such another?' was followed by the appearance of a star in the firmament – which reappeared when Brutus exclaims 'O Julius Caesar, thou art mighty yet.' Impressive, too, was Richard Johnson's Antony:

> Over six feet in height, darkly handsome, and a fine verse speaker, he gave the character an extraordinary physical and rhetorical magnetism. Antony's grief in the Senate was utterly unfeigned, and his determination to revenge, single-minded. In the Forum it was his passionate sincerity, rather than his tactics, which moved the mob. But once aware of his gifts as a spellbinder, latent vanity, ambition, and ruthlessness rapidly surfaced.[21]

An impressive and menacing Julius Caesar was at the heart of the RSC's productions of 1968 and 1972. In the former, directed by John Barton, Brewster Mason 'gave the play its heartbeat', gaining the initiative even at the moment of his death: 'Bearing down on Brutus as he fell, he seized with scorn the Stoic's faltering hand and forced the dagger home. His *"Et tu, Brute?"* was not a reproach, but a wrathful taunt.' Ian Richardson's Cassius also provided a 'compelling portrait':

> Obsessed by a lust for greatness, the febrile Roman found himself wanting when weighed on the Caesarian scale. The present standard of measurement, then, must be destroyed, and another set up more favourable to his gifts. His motivation seemed hardly more complex than that.[22]

As for Nunn's 1972 production, Mark Dignam as Caesar was 'the play's pivotal figure – a Fascist overreacher aspiring to divinity'. Here was:

an individual with no private self. Myth and man were one; and the effect was horrific. He bestrode the action of the early scenes like some omnipotent robot bent on subjugating every last vestige of individuality to the national will. At the same time he evinced a magnetism very nearly irresistible. One was forced to recognise his greatness, however malign; and one instantly understood Brutus' admiration for the man, and his reluctance to annihilate a veritable symbol of human potential. Although a bolder and less complex portrait than many of its predecessors, the impact of Dignam's Colossus was immediate, overwhelming, and all pervasive throughout.

But this production, presented together with *Antony and Cleopatra* and *Coriolanus* for only the second time in its stage history, contained other striking performances. John Wood's Brutus, for example, has been described as 'one of this century's most telling portraits of him'. In particular he seems to have conveyed an awareness of the profound anguish emanating from the duality of the public stoic and the strained private man. Richard Johnson's Antony was also a revelation:

> not so much a playboy or voluptuary as a black-bearded adventurer. He knew nothing of the moral turmoil of a Brutus or the psychological insecurities of a Cassius. He accepted the world as he found it, wresting from it as much as his strength and wits permitted. He was genuinely grieved by Caesar's death; but even as he lamented he weighed the opportunities for material advantage. Brutus and Cassius were easy prey to a man without either social needs or ethical scruples. The Forum speech was a supreme demonstration of how an individual unashamed of and unimpeded by his own passions could callously exploit those of others to serve his turn. In the end he met his match in Octavius (Corin Redgrave), the fair, clean-shaven, icy *arriviste*. With no feelings to be played upon, he offered Antony no target; and Antony's own passionate nature suddenly rendered him highly vulnerable. In the final moments of the play as Octavius froze Antony's sentimental elegy in mid-air, Antony realized he had been challenged to combat; and the choice of weapons was with the other side.[23]

A return to the suggestion of a fascist demagogue was apparent in the RSC's 1983 production directed by Ron Daniels. During the early part of the run Caesar was projected on to a huge screen at the back of the stage so that the actor was seen simultaneously life-sized in the foreground and colossal on the screen. This device (soon dropped for technical reasons) brought home to the audience the effectiveness of modern film and television techniques for elevating the personality of the dictator. But the very process of doing so coloured the attitude to Caesar. Once the equation is made with modern dictators, Shakespeare's ambivalent portrait is lost. A significant feature of this production was Emrys James' Cassius, who emerged as the most sympathetic character on the stage.

More neutral was the RSC's 1987 production directed by Terry Hands. Roger Allam was a highly sympathetic Brutus and Joseph O'Conor an attractive Caesar – interestingly, playing the role for the second consecutive Stratford production of the play. O'Conor, with his finely vigorous and mobile face, bald head and bright eyes, suggested a slightly fading vitality and acute intelligence becoming blurred with the development of self-aggrandising assertiveness. Here was a great man in the process of losing self-critical perceptiveness. O'Conor seemed able to attract and repel sympathy almost within the space of a sentence or a gesture. A striking feature of this production was the virtual absence of a stage crowd. During the Forum scene the audience was addressed directly while the noise of the crowd was intermittently projected by means of microphones. This technique was judged a failure and the absence of a stage crowd generated a feeling of the emptiness of Rome.

Consideration of past productions, only briefly sketched here, reveals the ways in which the interpretation of the play has varied according to the pressures of prevailing social and political circumstances and the predilections of actors and/or directors. *Julius Caesar* is a profoundly political play which quite naturally takes colour from the political tensions of the era and the society in which it is produced. But leaving aside such direct socio-political influences, its essentially enigmatic nature inevitably gives rise to differing perceptions. The quality an actor brings to any of the four major roles sets up a dynamic tension in terms of audience sympathy. To achieve their desired balance between characters, directors or actor-managers have generally resorted to cutting the text in order to preclude the undermining of their own prejudices (the frequent cutting in the past of the proscription scene is a notable example). Whereas Shakespeare presents us with a political dilemma complicated by the contradictory and paradoxical nature of human behaviour, few producers or directors have been willing to preserve such neutrality. A significant characteristic of the play is its diffusion of interest: it is possible for any one of the four major protagonists to gain audience sympathy; yet each character is given thoughts, expressions and actions which repel sympathy as powerfully as they attract it. If one character attains the stature of tragic hero, stage history suggests that that character is Marcus Brutus. However, this can be achieved unequivocally only by diminishing awkward or uncomfortable traits and by underplaying other characters. No matter how the play is weighted an uncut production will inevitably produce ambivalence, and a range of sympathies distributed, perhaps not evenly, between characters, so that *Julius Caesar* appears unlike *Hamlet* or *King Lear* for instance. Yet despite the the play's dispersal of emotional interest, it also seems to possess a dramatic texture quite different from the English history plays. History play, political play, tragedy – *Julius Caesar* seems to encompass all three types but ultimately is none of them. Simple yet complex, austere yet passionate, formal yet intimate, this play both in study and on the stage exhibits a unique dramatic dynamism which consistently stimulates, agitates and provokes conflicting intellectual and emotional responses. Extensive examination of the stage history of the play would serve merely to emphasise this internal dynamic and the kaleidescopic effects which it is capable of generating. But as John Ripley, author of the most extensive study of the play in performance, concludes:

> *Julius Caesar's* stage history, it must be acknowledged, is a tale of unrealized potential. To reveal itself fully the play requires an uncut text, fluid stagecraft, and actors of heroic power. And these three factors, sadly enough, have never conjoined. The eighteenth-century theatre played a relatively full text with flexible settings, but actors of mettle were few. The nineteenth-century stage, although graced with superb performers, mutilated the script, sacrificed ensemble effects to the star system, and hobbled the action by ponderous settings and business. The first half of this century saw the text restored and Elizabethan stagecraft rediscovered; but by then the classical acting tradition was almost extinct. In more recent times, although *Caesar* has been played whole, and for the most part fluidly, its splendour has gleamed only fitfully. Our leading players, like Garrick, Kean, and Irving before them, have shied at the play. Sir Laurence Olivier and Paul Schofield have never appeared in it; and Sir John Gielgud, a fine Antony and a brilliant Cassius, has not essayed Brutus, although the part might have been written for him. Good actors, if not the greatest, have attempted the major roles with some degree of ensemble; but their efforts have been frequently misdirected toward playing an interpretation rather than interpreting the play. Their directors, bent upon novelty and contemporary relevance, have all too often been less concerned with *Caesar* itself than a set of ideas about it.[24]

Before engaging in a deeper analysis of character and structure, the next logical move is to explore the social world which Shakespeare creates in this play. In whatever way directors and designers choose to present the play, they are confronted with a physical and social universe that is palpable. There is no getting away from this Rome. As one director, expressing his acceptance of contemporary settings for many of Shakespeare's plays, puts it:

> I would stop short at *Julius Caesar*. Why? As Rome is the hero of the piece, surely any production must present the city-state as Shakespeare very clearly drew it. To do otherwise is, for me, to remove the most important element of the piece and to artificially impose new concepts, which bear no relation to the playwright's original purpose.[25]

The Critical Reception

Shakespeare's Company, The Lord Chamberlain's Men, almost certainly chose *Julius Caesar* as the play to open their new Globe Theatre in 1599. They probably felt that here they had a subject with immediate box-office appeal. Julius Caesar and Brutus excited the popular imagination – their place in history, myth and literary tradition, and the partisan support which each enjoyed, was guaranteed to stimulate a lively interest in their presentation on the stage by the most popular dramatist of the day – an event not to be missed. Indeed, the play did achieve instant success and, with very few breaks, has held the stage ever since.

Some critics perceive the play as cold and static; others find the closing phase diffuse. Despite these criticisms, one simple fact cannot be denied – the consistent and widespread popularity of *Julius Caesar* from its earliest performances to the present day. It has thrilled and intrigued both popular audiences and scholars. Constantly provoking passionate debates about their essential natures, the roles of Antony, Brutus and Cassius have continued to exert a powerful attraction for actors. The part of Julius Caesar has not had anything like the same appeal, but interpretation of this role, too, has been subject to intense critical consideration with portrayals frequently reflecting prevailing social and political circumstances. The play's attractions and accessibility are revealed also by the place it has attained in the classroom. Ironically, this very popularity has brought about a tendency to devalue the play: it is frequently perceived as lacking the variety, subtlety and a richness of language realised in *Antony and Cleopatra* and the dramatic complexity and intensity of the four great tragedies. Yet, the enigmas of the play have kept critics busily attempting to answer such questions as: How does Shakespeare maintain the excitement and tension of the drama when the eponymous hero dies half-way through? What kind of man is Shakespeare's Julius Caesar? How noble, naïve or self-deceiving is Brutus? Where does the balance of sympathy lie between the contending forces? How and why does Shakespeare deviate from his source material? How has Shakespeare created such a powerful sense of a Roman world? What are the peculiar attributes of its language? What special quality creates a perception of both simplicity and complexity? Is it a history play or a tragedy? As one distinguished scholar puts it:

> *Julius Caesar* is one of Shakespeare's most controversial plays. Commentators have been quite unable to agree on who is its principal character or whether it has one; on whether it is a tragedy and, if so, of what kind; on whether Shakespeare wants us to consider the assassination as damnable or praiseworthy; while of all the chief characters in the play contradictory interpretations have been given.[1]

Within the Shakespearian canon the position of the play is, in itself, highly significant. Written at mid-point in his career, *Julius Caesar* is the gateway which separates the writing of the English histories from the great tragedies. Only two of Shakespeare's tragedies precede it – *Titus Andronicus* and *Romeo and Juliet*. Furthermore, it is the first play in which Shakespeare draws upon what was to prove an inspirational source – Thomas North's translation of Plutarch's *Lives of the Noble Grecians and Romans*.

There is general agreement that the play constitutes a watershed in Shakespeare's dramatic art. It is no exaggeration to claim, as Philip Brockbank has, that *Julius Caesar* marks 'a climactic point in the development of Shakespeare's art, in the history of theatre, and in the history of our consciousness of Rome'.[2] Warde Fowler,[3] Willard Farnham[4] and Virgil K. Whitaker[5] have also drawn attention to the innovative quality of the play, whereas Harley Granville-Barker has stressed the special challenge confronting Shakespeare in drawing upon the work of the great Greek historian – 'Plutarch gives him, not only the story he must abide by, but characters already charged with life' – and the success of the dramatist's response:

It is a feat of stagecraft to show us so many significant facets of this more than personal tragedy, a finer one to share out the best of the play's action among three chief characters and yet hardly lessen the strength of any of them.[6]

The last comment is particularly telling. The wide dispersal of emotional interest in *Julius Caesar* is unique in Shakespearian drama. One of the most persistent critical questions asked about the play is 'Who is the hero?' Brutus, Julius Caesar and Antony are all candidates for this title, and in the closing phase of the play, even minor characters, such as Messala and Titinius, achieve dramatic stature, thereby laying claim to our emotional and intellectual responses. This feature of the play has led many critics to complain about its diffuseness. Rejecting this criticism C. H. Herford claims:

> The structural mastery of the Roman plays is the more remarkable since he was here handling sources with far closer fidelity than before. In *Julius Caesar* above all, essential historicity was achieved without detriment to the most pellucid simplicity of structure.[7]

Julius Caesar, then, may well be labelled a simple play too complex for an entirely satisfactory interpretation. As G. Wilson Knight observed: 'The simplicity of *Julius Caesar* is a surface simplicity only. To close analysis it reveals subtleties and complexities which render interpretation difficult.'[8] Elusive is not the first word generally associated with *Julius Caesar*, yet everything about it is just that.

Shakespeare, when picking up his pen, had with him not only a volume of Plutarch, but also an awareness of the contrary attitudes adopted towards the central figures. Rather than taking up a position in this historical debate, the dramatist appears to have nurtured the ambiguities and un-certainties present in Plutarch. Occasionally, critics are unequivocal in their assessments of characters and their actions, but the intensity of the debates provoked by the play suggests that the uncertainties are as deeply ingrained in its structure as they are in the historical events recorded by Plutarch.

Not only is there acute critical disagreement about the characters, but the very structure of the play seems to invite discussion about precisely what kind of play it is. The eponymous hero dies half-way through yet his spirit haunts the rest of the action. It is Brutus who, like later tragic heroes, faces the central moral dilemma, and it is the interplay between Brutus' character and his actions that most fully engages the emotional and intellectual resources of the audience. Depending on the emphasis given to a production or the proclivities and experience of the reader, the play can be viewed as revenge tragedy or as a characteristically Shakespearian tragedy – if there is any such thing. However, neither of these perspectives focuses sufficiently on the play's political and historical features. *Julius Caesar* is very much concerned with the process by which individuals help shape history, are subject to its obscure but potent pressures, and see themselves as figures on the historical stage. Moreover, these characters do not operate against a vague background. Perhaps more powerfully than in any of his previous plays, Shakespeare creates an intense sense of a social universe: we feel and smell this Rome; we understand its values and the power exerted by its social ethos on the main protagonists. The play is infused with a sense of Rome: Roman landmarks, history, names and values are ubiquitous. And, for the first time, that essentially Roman character, the crowd, is given full voice, dominating both the opening scene and the play's most critical moment. This Rome is alive, throbbing with life, blood and sweat. It is elevated and dignified but it is also raucous and raw.

· 1 ·

Textual Issues

Julius Caesar was originally published in the First Folio of 1623. None of the subsequent quarto editions has any independent authority. Textual discussions of the play have been relatively free of complex debates because, as various editors of the play point out, 'there are fewer manifest corruptions than in any other play in the Folio'.[1] Moreover, the 'striking orderliness and clarity of presentation'[2] of the Folio text suggests that it was printed from a 'clean scribal transcript of Shakespeare's own working papers'.[3]

There are only four textual issues which have been subject to intense critical and editorial debate. Of these the least significant relates to the inconsistency several critics have detected in the character of Casca: they cannot be persuaded that the detached, cynical Casca of I.ii is the same character as the frightened rabbit of the storm scene (I.iii). John Dover Wilson[4] suggested that I.ii was written *after* I.iii and that Shakespeare never reconciled the two Cascas. The question is whether there *are* two incompatible Cascas or contrasting facets of the same character. A logical explanation is to accept that Casca in I.ii merely assumes the persona of the detached worldly-wise cynic and that underneath is the real Casca – a man terrified by what he sees as a portentous storm. This interpretation does not, however, commend itself to Granville-Barker:

1

We never see one flutter of that superficial garb of cynicism again. Casca remains hereafter the commonplace Casca of the storm-scene; the humorous blunt fellow seems forgotten quite. Certainly we have had Cassius' apology for him, that he

> puts on this tardy form . . .

But the passage in which that occurs is itself weak and mechanical, and it might arguably have been written in to excuse the clumsiness of the change.[5]

Norman Sanders is one of a few editors to uphold the psychological veracity of Casca: 'Casca, about whom Plutarch has only a handful of observations, comes to life in the play as a character as skilfully observed and psychologically credible as any minor figure in the Shakespeare canon.'[6]

The second textual problem concerns the replacement of Cassius by Publius when the conspirators visit Caesar. Wilson suggested that the same actor played 'lean' Cassius and 'lean' Ligarius, so that the producer resolved the dilemma by substituting Publius for Cassius.[7] An audience would certainly not have time to notice Cassius' absence, so this may well have been an adroit solution to a technical problem. Subsequently, however, some critics have advanced other reasons for the absence of Cassius among his fellow conspirators on that fateful morning. Could he not face up to the required hypocrisy? Was his antagonism towards Caesar so obvious that his appearance might arouse suspicion? While it is hardly possible to be sure what was intended, it is worth remembering that the absence of Cassius among the conspirators in this scene does not strike the audience – only the very careful reader. If the exclusion of Cassius is deliberate, the dramatist provided no markers to attract the attention of the audience to his absence.

The third issue relates to Ben Jonson's jibe that:

> Many times he [Shakespeare] fell into those things, could not escape laughter: As when he said in the person of *Caesar*, one speaking to him; 'Caesar, thou dost me wrong'. He replied: 'Caesar did never wrong, but with just cause': and such like; which were ridiculous.[8]

The quotation comes from Jonson's *Discoveries*, published posthumously, but compiled mainly between 1626 and 1637. The accuracy of Jonson's quotation is generally accepted because he was noted for his good memory.

Moreover, he would hardly be likely to misquote something which could easily be refuted by reference to the First Folio. The assumption is that what Jonson quoted was what Shakespeare wrote and that what appears in the First Folio is the result of emendation by the editors in response to Jonson's ridicule – something not confined to the *Discoveries*. There is an allusion to the line in Jonson's *The Staple of News* played in 1626 and contained in the printed text of 1631. *The Induction* contains the following exchange, evidently intended to raise a laugh:

> *Expectation* *I can do that too, if I have cause.*
> *Prologue* *Cry you mercy*, you never did wrong, but with just cause.

The different typeface indicates that a quotation was intended. All this could be dismissed as much ado about nothing, were it not for the fact that it raises a substantive point of critical significance. Perhaps the best gloss has been provided by John Palmer, who comments:

> The folio text gives to Caesar at the conclusion of the speech in which he rejects Cimber's appeal a comparatively tame remark which, in the circumstances, is dramatically irrelevant:
>
> > Know, Caesar doth not wrong, nor without cause
> > Will he be satisfied.
>
> There can be no reasonable doubt of the true reading. Jonson's version is dramatic, significant and in character. The folio version is insipid, superfluous and out of character not only with Shakespeare's presentation of Caesar as a whole but with the particular scene which is taking place. Caesar has just insisted that nothing will move him from his purpose. Was he likely to conclude upon a non-sequitur which suggests that he might be satisfied if cause were shown? . . .
>
> *Caesar did never wrong but with just cause* – it is Shakespeare's finishing touch to the portrait of a dictator. It is the last, if it be not also the first, assumption of the man who lives for power that the wrong he does is right.[9]

Wilson has added a significant comment on Jonson's version of this disputed line: 'Its very isolation and abruptness give it just that hint of menace and air of inflexible finality which the end of such a speech demands.'[10] These two are among a number of distinguished critics who

believe that what Jonson recorded was what Shakespeare wrote and that
the Folio editors amended the text in the light of the criticism. Whatever
the truth of the matter, there can be little doubt that the Jonson version is
much more potent than its Folio counterpart.

The fourth textual problem, and by far the most important, relates to the
double announcement of Portia's death during the quarrel scene (IV.iii). As
the text stands, the conclusion of the quarrel between Brutus and Cassius,
and the ejection of the cynic poet, leads to the following exchange:

Bru.	Lucius, a bowl of wine.
	[*Exit Lucius.*]

Cas. I did not think you could have been so angry.

Bru. O Cassius, I am sick of many griefs.

Cas. Of your philosophy you make no use,
        If you give place to accidental evils.

Bru. No man bears sorrow better. Portia is dead.

Cas. Ha? Portia?

Bru. She is dead.

Cas. How 'scap'd I killing, when I cross'd you so?
        O insupportable and touching loss!
        Upon what sickness?

Bru.   Impatient of my absence,
        And grief that young Octavius with Mark Antony
        Have made themselves so strong; for with her death
        That tidings came. With this she fell distract,
        And, her attendants absent, swallow'd fire.

Cas. And died so?

Bru.   Even so.

Cas.   O ye immortal gods!
        Enter boy [LUCIUS] *with wine and tapers.*

Bru. Speak no more of her. Give me a bowl of wine.
        In this I bury all unkindness Cassius.   [*Drinks.*]

Cas. My heart is thirsty for that noble pledge.
        Fill, Lucius, till the wine o'erswell the cup.
        I cannot drink too much of Brutus' love.
                                [*Exit Lucius.*]
                        [*Enter* TITINIUS *and* MESSALA.]

Bru. Come in, Titinius. Welcome, good Messala.
        Now sit we close about this taper here,
        And call in question our necessities.

Cas. Portia, art thou gone?

Bru.	No more, I pray you.
	Messala, I have here received letters,
	That young Octavius and Mark Antony
	Come down upon us with a mighty power,
	Bending their expedition toward Philippi.
Mes.	Myself have letters of the self-same tenor.
Bru.	With what addition?
Mes.	That by proscription and bills of outlawry
	Octavius, Antony, and Lepidus
	Have put to death an hundred senators.
Bru.	Therein our letters do not well agree.
	Mine speak of seventy senators that died
	Bt their proscriptions, Cicero being one.
Cas.	Cicero one?
Mes.	Cicero is dead,
	And by that order of proscription.
	Had you your letters from your wife, my lord?
Bru.	No, Messala.
Mes.	Nor nothing in your letters writ of her?
Bru.	Nothing, Messala.
Mes.	That, methinks, is strange.
Bru.	Why ask you? Hear you aught of her in yours?
Mes.	No, my lord.
Bru.	Now as you are a Roman, tell me true.
Mes.	Then like a Roman bear the truth I tell;
	For certain she is dead, and by strange manner.
Bru.	Why, farewell, Portia. We must die, Messala.
	With meditating that she must die once,
	I have the patience to endure it now.
Mes.	Even so great men great losses should endure.
Cas.	I have as much of this in art as you,
	But yet my nature could not bear it so.
Bru.	Well, to our work alive. What do you think
	Of marching to Philippi presently?

(IV.iii.141–96)

There has been a torrent of critical opinion denouncing Brutus for lying to Messala, by claiming ignorance of Portia's death, and then exhibiting stoic fortitude. The general feeling is that the incident is so damaging to Brutus' character that what we have in the Folio text is a corruption; the theory being that the dramatist originally wrote only the second disclosure (Brutus is not, therefore, guilty of an untruth), but that this presented Brutus as excessively cold and unfeeling, and so he replaced it with the first confession. This had the additional virtue of softening audience hostility towards Brutus created by his treatment of Cassius, and it also made for a natural process of reconciliation, but somehow the two announcements became incorporated into the Folio text. This reasoning is very attractive to those who feel that the Folio text, as it stands, is more damaging to the character of Brutus than the dramatist intended, and, indeed, for some time bibliographical and typographical 'proof' was cited to justify the argument. This evidence, however, has since been shown to be suspect and so the argument once more rests on critical grounds.[11]

Before attempting to offer an opinion on this contentious matter, it is worth noting that Harley Granville-Barker[12] subscribes to the revised version theory and receives tentative support from Arthur Humphries,[13] the editor of the recent Oxford edition of the play. One of the significant features of the latter's judicious summary, however, is his reference to the successful playing of the text as we have it. It would appear that the discomfort felt by the critic in the study is not experienced in the theatre, which may be enough to cast doubt on the revised text theory. Moreover, not all critics subscribe to the view that Brutus' response to Messala is unworthy or, to put it more strongly, that it 'takes his display of self-command to the point of caricature'.[14] John Palmer sees the incident as a fundamental expression of Brutus' dilemma in the play: 'Brutus may be playing a part, but it is one which springs from the fundamental lie in his character, the lie that impels him to substitute a public figure for the natural man.'[15] This interpretation shows Brutus not to be putting on a show of stoicism for purposes of self-aggrandisement, but following through his adopted role as servant of the republic even though his words and actions work against the grain of his feelings. Indeed, the ebb and flow of tension and emotion in the scene are such that the Folio text feels right.

Two critics who have recently adopted a similar line of reasoning to Palmer's are Brents Stirling[16] and A. D. Nuttall. The latter sums up his view of the revised text theory by stating that: 'To take this course at one stroke removes both the difficulties and the tense excitement of the scene.'[17] It is not necessary to accept the precise details of any one interpretation to appreciate that the double announcement may well have been quite deliberate by Shakespeare. Muir, for example, argues that:

> If Messala's account was ever the only one, it is odd that Brutus should not ask Messala to enlarge upon the strange manner of Portia's death; and if, in fact, some lines have been deleted at this point, it is odd

that the whole episode was not cut. One is driven to assume that Shakespeare intended the duplicate revelation to stand.[18]

There seems little to add to this impeccable logic, but recently Thomas Healy has argued that the whole conception of the double announcement arose from the interpretive predilections of several editors and critics:

> The actions of editorial emendation in this instance worked to suppress the scene's representation of Brutus as a role player. As Cassius remarks when Brutus has impressed the officers of his stoical resolve in accepting Portia's death: 'I have as much of this in art as you,/But yet my nature could not bear it so' (IV.iii. 192–3). Cassius is interested, too, in role-playing but is less successful at it than Brutus. The scene does not necessarily present Brutus in an unfavourable light. His collected resolve in front of his officers is assuring his troops' confidence in his controlled capacity to lead them as they prepare for an impending battle. His action as a general is sensible. But what was clear is that the editors, believing that the play was about the intrinsically moral Brutus, could not accept a feigning Brutus and so explained away, or repressed, the scene where that role-playing is most formally represented. Believing that tragic greatness was founded on an exploration of a great individual, the literary institution found ways of assuring that Shakespeare's plays observed their premises. What could not be allowed was the suggestion that major characters were using language to deceive and self-present in expedient ways which suited political needs rather than the way they 'really were'.[19]

Healy, whether or not one agrees with his interpretation of the scene, is making a valuable point by revealing how editorial emendation or commentary can arise from, and subsequently influence, critical interpretation – a point made with great vigour by Ann Thompson in connection with the editorial glosses on Casca's comment that 'Marullus and Flavius, for pulling scarfs off Caesar's images, are put to silence' (I.ii.282–3).[20]

This scene, which has long been acclaimed as one of the most exciting and moving in the play, exhibits a fascinating interplay between naked human emotion under stress and an endeavour to achieve controlled, dignified behaviour. Removing Messala's announcement, and its consequent reverberations, *may* make for greater clarity, but only at the expense of authentic and fascinating dramatic complexity.

Finally, a brief comment is necessary on a few lines which critics and editors have found ambiguous. Cassius' words at the end of the seduction scene are:

Well, Brutus, thou art noble; yet I see
Thy honourable mettle may be wrought
From that it is dispos'd: therefore 'tis meet
That noble minds keep ever with their likes;
For who so firm that cannot be seduc'd?
                                    (I.ii.305–9)

Norman Sanders, a particularly clear-sighted editor comments:

> Many critics of the play have argued that, in this speech, Cassius is
> referring not to his own practice on Brutus, which we have just wit-
> nessed, but to Caesar's possible seduction of Brutus by favours and
> tyrannical influence. . . . While it is impossible to prove that such an
> interpretation as this is wrong, it is nevertheless improbable, both
> because it depends on an awkward grammatical construction which, in
> the theatre, would almost certainly not convey the meaning required,
> and because it relies on a knowledge of material not contained in the
> play (an un-Shakespearian dramatic practice).[21]

It may be added that the interpretation favoured by Sanders is more in
accord with the character of Cassius. The lines following those previously
cited –

Caesar doth bear me hard; but he loves Brutus.
If I were Brutus now, and he were Cassius,
He should not humour me.
                                    (I.ii.310–12)

– imply that were he the recipient of Caesar's love he could never be
persuaded to act against him. There is an irony in this interpretation of
character, in that the politically aware and guileful Cassius recognises
something fundamental in his own nature (a predilection to put personal
affection before principles), but he is unaware of how this will make him
vulnerable to Brutus' influence, whose public image is necessary to the
conspiracy but whose political and military decision-making is fatally
flawed from the outset. Cassius is never able to resist his esteemed friend:
his acceptance of Brutus' moral superiority, along with his yearning for
Brutus' love, stop him asserting his superior political and military judgement. The irony of this speech, then, has far more interest than has been
allowed by critics who have focused primarily on its ambiguity.[22]

· 2 ·

Genre and Unity: What Kind of Play is *Julius Caesar*?

Ever since the Roman plays were included among the tragedies in the First Folio there has been a tendency to view them through the same lens as that applied to the 'great four' tragedies. Dissatisfaction with this perspective has grown in recent years and is reflected in such works as John Wilders' *The Lost Garden: A view of Shakespeare's English and Roman history plays* (1978) and Alexander Leggatt's *Shakespeare's Political Drama: The history plays and the Roman plays* (1988). These critics perceive powerful connections between the Roman plays and the English histories. The Roman plays are history plays and political plays as well as being tragedies – which gives rise to the question: can any useful distinction be made between a history play and a tragedy? One thing the plays have in common is that they are based on what Shakespeare believed to be historical fact – though he doubtless recognised the differences in quality of the historical materials with which he dealt.[1] John Wilders suggests that at one level the distinction between the histories and tragedies is at the very least blurred:

> The only immediately obvious feature which the histories have in common is that they all deal with the history of England. A case could be made for describing some of Heminge's and Condell's 'histories' as 'tragedies', particularly *Richard II* and *Richard III*, both of which have

dominant heroes and are distinguished from the other histories in the table of contents by the description '*The Life and Death*'. Again, some of the Folio tragedies could well be considered histories: *Julius Caesar* has no central, commanding hero of the magnitude of Hamlet or Macbeth and this play, too, is described as '*The Life and Death*' *of Julius Caesar*. The superficial evidence suggests, then, that the distinction between Shakespeare's histories and his tragedies is not as clear-cut as the Folio division implies.

Having cast doubt on the merit of treating these groups of plays as separate entities, Wilders observes that there is one very important sense in which the histories and tragedies differ from each other:

> The difference seems to lie in the role of the tragic hero. Whereas a history play portrays the fortunes of many characters as they play their roles in a nation's continuing life, a tragedy is devoted chiefly to the struggles of one character, and his death, depicted as the outcome of the conflicts which occupy the play, gives to the ending of a tragedy a sense of absolute finality. A Shakespearean tragedy has what Peter Ure calls 'the order and unity of biography', a unity implied by the old title '*The Life and Death*'. But whereas the death of a tragic hero conveys a sense of an ending, the impression created by a history play is that the life of a nation has neither beginning nor ending.[2]

This very useful distinction enables us to draw a fairly clear line between such plays as *Hamlet* and *King Lear* on the one hand and the plays in the history cycles and even *King John* and *Henry VIII* on the other. Application of this criterion to the Roman plays reveals the extent to which their historical dimension transcends that of the other plays traditionally categorised as tragedies. It is not merely a sense of historical continuity which the Roman plays share with the English histories: they also create an awareness of a political identity, institutions and conflicts.

Kenneth Muir maintains that there is 'no evidence that Shakespeare regarded the Roman plays as different *in kind* from the other tragedies'.[3] Nevertheless, there are three reasons for making a distinction between the histories and the tragedies. First, Shakespearian tragedies leave us with a profound sense of finality, whereas the history plays convey a sense of continuity. Our attention in the histories is divided (though not equally) between the stopping-point at the end of the play and anticipation of the future. At the end of the tragedies we are not concerned with the future: beyond the events we have experienced, the future seems insubstantial and irrelevant. The questions provoked by the action are the large philosophical issues about the nature of man in the universe. (Though acute questioning of the nature of authority and political institutions in *King Lear*, for example, as Dollimore and R. S. White have shown, is not precluded.[4])

Secondly, there is a dispersal of emotional involvement in the history plays. The stage history of *Julius Caesar* suggests that it is *the* most striking example of emotional dispersal – Brutus, Antony and even Cassius have, at times, been accorded the status of 'hero', each having emerged as the most sympathetic character in the play. The editor of the New Cambridge edition of the play makes a strong case for regarding Brutus as the hero of the piece,[5] whereas Clifford Leech has expressed the view that 'Brutus does not really occupy the hero's part'.[6] Irving Ribner claims that: 'The fate of Brutus or Caesar is secondary to that of Rome',[7] while Reuben Brower also concludes that in *Julius Caesar* Shakespeare 'has made a commitment not to a tragedy of the sort he will write later, but to a "*noble* Roman history"'.[8] Even Antony and Cleopatra do not dominate their play as do Othello, Hamlet, Lear, Macbeth and Timon. The heroes of the tragedies have a self-obsessive quality which draws the audience into a journey through the landscape of the mind. The catalyst, be it 'filial ingratitude', betrayal or ambition, paradoxically leads to a contraction of the central character's area of interest while simultaneously expanding audience consciousness of matters cosmic and universal. There is a contrasting perspective in the Roman plays: Arthur Humphries comments that what characters 'find out about themselves in the tragic action is not some new moral dimension, a discovered world within, but how their code enables them to face success or failure'.[9] John Bayley expresses the distinction in a slightly different form: 'In the tragedies of consciousness inner being grows and intensifies: in the Roman tragedies the external self stands up to the end, until it is struck down or strikes down itself.'[10]

Thirdly, and perhaps most importantly, the Roman plays are culturally specific in a sense which does not apply to any of the other tragedies. This is not to imply that Shakespeare fails to create a sense of a social universe in the other tragedies, but that these social worlds are not so individual that they cannot transfer to different times and places without severe dislocation. In a radio broadcast (BBC, 21 May 1989) David Daniell commented on the way in which Shakespeare seems to have 'flattened the background of Timon's Athens'. This is in no way true of the Roman worlds. More than any other group of plays, or any individual play, they create an intense sense of a social universe – not just a sense of place but an awareness of the values, attitudes, aspirations and idiosyncrasies of the different Romes which are portrayed in *Titus Andronicus, Julius Caesar, Antony and Cleopatra* and *Coriolanus*. Shakespeare gives a palpable sense of a Roman world in diverse ways: the physical landmarks of Rome, such as the Tiber and the Capitol, are mentioned with great frequency; there are many references to Roman manners and customs – the feast of Lupercal in the opening scenes of *Julius Caesar* for example; political and religious institutions and officials (such as tribunes, aediles, patricians, augurers, flamens – priests – or lictors – ushers) are ever present; the mythology of the pantheon and references to the gods pervade the plays; and Roman history, including most vitally its Trojan origins, is focused in the minds of the major participants. Yet, when all this is recognised, the most important reason for feeling such an intense awareness of the peculiar quality of these societies is through the articulation of Roman values. These values are not platitudinous precepts but deeply held convictions about the relative worth of different kinds of human activity. Referring to the concepts of nobility and honour, Humphries points out that:

> Throughout North's Plutarch the word 'noble' sounds recurrently, often for prowess in war . . . but often carrying also the sense of moral beauty. . . . In the English histories honour and glory are frequently objects of aspiration; in the Roman ones they are the presiding values, coupled with the idea of the noble, a word ranging from the self-assertion of a Coriolanus to the disinterested idealism of a Brutus.[11]

The central values of Shakespeare's Roman worlds are service to the state, constancy, fortitude, valour, friendship, love of family and respect for the gods. The relative importance attaching to these values varies from play to play because Shakespeare portrays a changing Rome. Even though the relative importance accorded to each of these values changes through time, they all continue to shape perceptions and are persistently invoked to commend or condemn human behaviour. Indeed, the catalyst for conflict is always the collision of values or a divergence between personal aspirations and obligation to the society. Thus it is not only a sense of historical continuity which the Roman plays share with the English histories, but also a distinct feeling of political identity, institutions and conflicts. If the identity of England as a place and a symbol is clearly articulated in Shakespeare's ten history plays, the sense of Rome as place and symbol is even more powerfully emphasised in the four Roman plays.

The sense of Rome as an historical entity redolent with suggestion has received careful consideration from Robert S. Miola, who, in *Shakespeare's Rome*, maintains that Rome:

is sometimes metaphor, sometimes myth, sometimes both, sometimes neither. Despite its metamorphoses, Rome maintains a distinct identity. Constructed of forums, walls, and Capitol, opposed to outlying battle-fields, wild, primitive landscapes, and enemy cities, Rome is a palpable though ever-changing presence. The city serves not only as a setting for action, but also as central protagonist. Embodying the heroic traditions of the past, Rome shapes its inhabitants, who often live or die according to its dictates for the approval of its future generations.

Miola has a keen sense of the shaping power of Rome, of its multifarious associations and of the influence exerted by its values, and of its en-trenched sense of destiny. For him, 'constancy, honour and *pietas* (the loving respect owed to family, country, and gods)'[12] are the central Roman ideals. In a fascinating article, John W. Velz examines the authenticity of Shakespeare's portrayal of the city by focusing on its architecture and its separation as an urban centre, both physically and symbolically, from the rural hinterland:

> Whatever the limitations of his detailed knowledge of buildings, Shake-speare thought of Rome in architectural terms. . . . The city is also to Shakespeare a set of psychologically significant, virtually symbolic, loci often placed in contrast with one another – the Forum, the battlefield, the Senate house, the street, the domicile. Each is a manifestation of *Romanitas*, the domicile not less than public buildings, for it is in the Roman plays that Shakespeare most powerfully contrasts public and private life, portraying them sometimes as mutually inimical.

> The most important edifice in Shakespeare's Rome, its wall, is seldom spoken of by scholars. To Shakespeare Rome is above all *urbs* in its etymological sense, the enclave of civilization ringed round with a protective wall, outside of which the dark forces of barbarism lurk. . . . The wall of Rome encloses a *polis* which in its political and social decorum embodies civilization.[13]

Many critics have, of course, drawn attention to what they see as 'lapses' in Shakespeare's portrayal of Rome. Paradoxically, it is the co-mingling of Roman and Elizabethan worlds which gives the Roman plays such an intense feeling of social reality. In comparing Shakespeare with Jonson, Charles and Michelle Martindale point out that 'Shakespeare has a lighter touch with his Roman details', going on to argue that: 'What differen-tiates Shakespeare's treatment from the norm is not so much a superior intellectual understanding of ancient conceptions, but a more complex dramatic technique in exhibiting them.' Moreover, turning specifically to the question of such anachronisms as sweaty nightcaps and Caesar's doublet, these authors advance a number of arguments that justify Shakespeare's practice in the light of prevailing artistic attitudes:

> In discussing the question of the 'truth' of poetry, most (following Aristotle) agreed that it consisted not in minute factual accuracy but in verisimilitude. Anachronisms could be justified as a means of bringing the past to life and making the representation convincing to the audience. . . . Anachronism was also sanctioned by the practice of Roman poets like Virgil, who included in the *Aeneid* customs and objects which clearly did not belong to the heroic world of primitive Italy that he was describing.[14]

What Shakespeare does in each of the Roman plays is to give us a vision of a society which is so infused with its value system that characters interact not merely with each other but with the history, goals and aspirations of Rome. Cicero's enunciation of the fundamental principle of Roman citizenship, 'This, then, ought to be the chief end of all men, to make the interest of each individual and of the whole body politic identical',[15] would not have been challenged. Of course, as the circumstances of Rome changed so too did the best way of serving the state – something clearly reflected in the plays. The primitive Rome of *Coriolanus* (494–91 BC) has acquired a sense of identity, of superiority even, but the precariousness of its position is manifest, and so physical courage is the most effective way of serving the state. As Cominius makes the point:

> It is held
> That valour is the chiefest virtue and
> Most dignifies the haver:
> (II.ii.83–5)

When we move to the Rome of *Julius Caesar* (45–42 BC) a sense of service to the state is again powerfully articulated by Brutus:

> If it be ought toward the general good,
> Set honour in one eye, and death i'th'other,
> And I will look on both indifferently;
> For let the gods so speed me as I love
> The name of honour more than I fear death.
> (I.ii.84–8)

Once more service to the society is the supreme value transcending the importance of life itself; but 'honour' here is not essentially a matter of physical courage. Brutus and Cassius have to take to the battlefield, but the whole feel of the play is that public service is expressed, primarily, by participation in the councils of state. Indeed, the central issue of the play revolves around the threat by Caesar to usurp the power of these institutions, thereby denying the very means of service and honour. This Rome is politically mature with a sophisticated culture and a proud history. Cicero, the powerful orator and statesman, makes a brief appearance; Cato's greatness is invoked; Lucius Junius Brutus' legendary feat of freeing Rome from the last of its kings constitutes a critical element in the emotional pressure of events; and Cassius, when describing his rescue of Caesar from the Tiber, registers the unbroken history of Rome from its very foundation:

> I, as Aeneas, our great ancestor,
> Did from the flames of Troy upon his shoulder
> The old Anchises bear, so from the waves of Tiber
> Did I the tired Caesar.
>
> (I.ii.111–14)

Here, then, is a self-conscious Rome: a society aware of its past as a living organism, a source of strength essential to its very existence. Achievements and ideals impose moral imperatives, but there is a sense that the Roman ethos is being threatened. There can be no Rome 'When there is in it but one only man' (I.ii.155). Julius Caesar is perceived as constituting a threat not only to political expression but to the concept that is Rome.

The celebration which opens the play signifies not a victory over foreigners but Caesar's triumph over fellow Romans – sons of the legendary Pompey. Flavius and Marullus immediately introduce us to a world of political conflict. But they are not merely political opponents of Caesar, they are passionately opposed to the concept of Caesarism which to them is a denial of the meaning of Rome as a living principle. The plebeians, contented and footloose, are outsiders, observers of the political process who become insiders only during political crises. They have been absorbed into the body politic while being simultaneously neutralised. The cobbler baits his social superior with impunity, suggesting a considerable degree of social freedom – surely the primary point Shakespeare wishes to convey through the cobbler's banter (but see Toole's fascinating discussion).[16] In this mature Rome political conflict is not between patrician and plebeian but is within the patrician class. With this political maturity there is a subtle undermining of Roman values. This is a world where Roman values still exert a powerful influence, but personal antagonisms and political ambitions break through the fabric. Brutus is drawn into the conspiracy because his reputation as a man of integrity will serve to provide political credibility to the conspirators. This reveals that values still count but that they are subject to manipulation by ambitious men (for instance, the 'popular appeal' to Brutus is forged by Cassius). The proscription scene is stunning in its display of political cynicism: a death list of political adversaries is drawn up in a cold and brutal way with relatives' lives bargained to buy the deaths of personal rivals; Caesar's will is distorted to raise funds; and Lepidus is drawn in as a make-weight to deflect opprobrium from Antony and Octavius – who clearly intend to remove him when the time is ripe.

Thus Shakespeare's creation of a pulsating Roman world gives to *Julius Caesar* a powerful unity that distinguishes it from the tragedies. The dispersal of emotional interest and the play's sense of continuity rather than finality gives it a kinship with the English histories, but *Julius Caesar* stands out as something new and different from everything that precedes it. Although recognition of the authenticity and potency of Shakespeare's Rome only gradually achieved critical recognition, appreciation of the play's originality goes back a long way and raised important considerations about its unity.

W. Warde Fowler emphasised the originality of the play but suggested that its innovative quality gave rise to a difficulty which the dramatist failed to resolve:

> We have in fact in *Julius Caesar* the meeting-point of the old and the new ideas of tragedy. We have the sudden fall of a man of overwhelming greatness – this was the old idea, of which Marlowe's *Tamburlaine* may be cited as the type; and at the same time we have retribution falling upon a good man whose very goodness has made him wrong-headed in action – this is the new idea, which could be used in various ways in the tragedies that were to follow. The result on the play of this compromise between the old and the new is not wholly to its advantage. It falls too clearly into two parts, and neither part is perfect. A play with a double plan of construction, in which the crisis overbears the catastrophe in interest, must have given its author unusual trouble.[17]

Willard Farnham also stressed the way in which Shakespeare breaks new ground by creating a tragedy which becomes the precursor of later and greater tragedies:

Julius Caesar is a landmark not merely in the history of Shakespearean tragedy but in the history of English tragedy. Before Brutus there had been no tragic hero on the English stage whose character had combined noble grandeur with fatal imperfection. . . . In Brutus, then, Shakespeare discovered the noble hero with a tragic flaw. By that discovery he made it possible for English tragedy to reach a greatness hitherto attained only by Greek tragedy.[18]

For these critics, then, *Julius Caesar* is a seminal tragedy – but this view did not enjoy universal assent. There were many who adopted the stance of H. B. Charlton, seeing Brutus as 'no more significant in the play than is Hotspur in *Henry IV*' so that 'it is impossible to fit *Julius Caesar* into Shakespeare's mode of tragedy'.[19] Wilson was also keenly aware of the dispersal of interest, claiming that 'the main issue of the play is not the conspirators' fate but the future of Rome, of liberty, of the human race, to which their fate is incidental'.[20] Ernest Schanzer, however, has taken strong issue with this approach, insisting that:

The main issue of *Julius Caesar*, as I see it, is not a political but a moral issue, consisting in the conflicting claims of the realm of personal relations and that of politics. . . .
Its central character is Brutus, in whom the moral issue is fought out, and whose tragedy . . . is very much of the Shakespearian kind. It is on Brutus, the only person in the play who experiences any inner conflict, that our main interest is focussed from the first, and it is with an eye on him that much of the play's material is presented.

But, having put forward a persuasive argument for viewing the play as a Shakespearian tragedy with Brutus as the tragic hero, Schanzer muddies the water by adding a complicating footnote:

as a tragedy *Julius Caesar* belongs with Shakespeare's mature tragedies in its emphasis on Brutus's tragic experience and in the form which this experience takes . . . it is, indeed, the first of the tragedies to exhibit this characteristically Shakespearian pattern . . . it especially points forward to *Macbeth* . . . in this play Shakespeare put a twofold problem before his audience: the psychological problem of the nature of the 'real' Caesar; and, hinging upon this, the moral problem of the justifiability of the murder . . . by the orientation of his material Shakespeare deliberately avoided giving a plain and clear-cut answer to either of these problems . . . *Julius Caesar* is therefore one of Shakespeare's few genuine problem plays.[21]

It is, of course, possible to accept the general thrust of Schanzer's comments on the play without agreeing that it is best viewed as a 'problem play'.

Another perspective on the play has been provided by those who see it as
a tragedy, but of a very special kind. The case for seeing the play as an
example of that most popular of Elizabethan and Jacobean tragedies, the
revenge play, has been expressed most persuasively by Norman Rabkin. He
makes the point that the critical moment of Antony's revenge speech
changes the nature of the play:

> Mark Antony here calls up the world of revenge tragedy. No member of
> an audience remembering the *Ur-Hamlet* and *Titus Andronicus*, still in
> love with *The Spanish Tragedy* and within a year of seeing the first
> performance of *Hamlet*, could have missed Shakespeare's point. . . . In
> the bloody world of revenge tragedy an audience knows precisely how to
> evaluate the part of each actor: Brutus, the first criminal, who must trade
> his life for his crime; Mark Antony, the hero-revenger, who is no sooner
> a hero than by the inner dynamics of his role he is the villain of the piece.
>
> The logic of the revenge conventions justifies the title of a play in
> which the titular hero is out of the way before the third Act has barely got
> under way: Caesar is the moving force of the tragedy. The action of the
> play makes clear sense in terms of revenge tragedy.[22]

Rabkin is surely right in claiming that the Elizabethan audience would
immediately have recognised the revenge tragedy pattern in the play, but it
is a giant step from there to assert that Shakespeare's audience would
have perceived the play simply as a revenge tragedy. The powerful echo
of revenge tragedy would certainly have been one important source of
dramatic unity but consciousness of other significant elements in the play
would have precluded such an uncomplicated response.

The potency of the revenge tragedy dimension of the play has been
emphasised by Nicholas Brooke, who recognises 'a quality in the play
which exceeds its simple framework and is not reconciled with it'.[23] Like
Brooke, James C. Bulman has highlighted the revenge tragedy aspect of the
play, but unlike Brooke he sees Shakespeare consciously and *successfully*
absorbing it within a wider framework.[24] An indication of the felt presence
of the revenge tragedy quality of the play can be derived from W. Nicholas
Knight's fascinating article 'Brutus' motivation and melancholy'. Knight is
unorthodox in that Brutus, rather than Mark Antony, is seen as the
revenger. As he puts it: 'a number of stage conventions and a close analysis
of the symptoms and diagnosis of Brutus' malady in *Julius Caesar* suggest
that "the mad Brutus" does fall into the category of the conventional

Elizabethan revenge hero'.[25] This unusual perspective on the revenge hero is shared by Alan Hager, who provides a detailed elucidation of the idea:

> In Elizabethan revenge tragedy, the ghost of the prior victim may appear not in front of his murderer, like Macbeth, but strictly in front of his avenger, like Hamlet. Caesar's ghost appears to both in the same person. Brutus will simultaneously become Caesar's avenger and his punished murderer in his own suicide – and by the same sword. His identity here with Caesar will be final and complete. The man who sacrificed Caesar will be sacrificed as the man who sacrificed Pompey was sacrificed.[26]

It is not possible to know why Shakespeare made such use of the revenge tragedy motif in the play, but Robert S. Miola makes an interesting suggestion based on an earlier observation by Warde Fowler. He cites a passage from Plutarch which may have inspired Shakespeare: 'But his [Caesar's] great prosperitie and good fortune that favoured him all his life time, did continue afterwards in the revenge of his death, pursuing the murtherers both by sea and land, till they had not left a man more to be executed.' Thus Miola observes: 'Herein are two seminal conceptions for Shakespeare, particularly for acts 4 and 5: the notion that Caesar (or part of him) lives on after death; the idea that Roman history works like a revenge tragedy.'[27] For Miola, then, the inspiration for utilising the revenge tragedy structure comes directly from Plutarch. Arthur Humphries also draws attention to the influence exerted by Plutarch on the structure of the play, commenting that:

> Over and above the details of history it is this Plutarchan sense of retributive destiny which gives the play its unity, Caesar's death being the keystone of the great arch which brings the conspirators up to their triumph and down to their doom.[28]

Despite these comments on its structural unity one persistent criticism of *Julius Caesar* is that it peters out after the tremendous excitement of the Forum scene. However, the critical assertion of the thematic and structural unity of the play is much stronger than the countervailing tendency. L. C. Knights, for instance, insists that 'the play forms a coherent and tightly woven whole', adding: 'There is no question here of a broken-backed play in which flagging interest must be maintained by adventitious means. The play is as much of a unity as *Macbeth*.'[29]

Another approach to this question is that adopted by Brents Stirling, who shows how ceremony is a vital structural element in unifying the play, with each ceremony having a counterpart which generally contradicts its meaning or significance:

> In the first scene the tribunes denounce the punctilio planned for Caesar's entry, send the idolatrous crowd to rites of purification, and set off themselves to desecrate the devotional images. In the second scene a multiple emphasis of ceremony is capped by Casca's satire which twists the crown ritual into imbecile mummery.

Likewise, Brutus' ritualisation of the assassination is later inverted by Antony. In displaying Caesar's torn and bloodied robe during his Forum speech:

> Antony re-enacts the death of Caesar in a ritual of his own, one intended to show that the original 'lofty scene' presented a base carnage . . . his recreation of the rite becomes a mockery of it. Brutus' transformation of blood into the heady wine of sacrifice is reversed both in substance and in ceremony.[30]

By drawing attention to the key structural pressure points of the action Geoffrey Bullough has also suggested a structural unity in the play:

> In action *Julius Caesar* is a tragic chronicle with three main foci: the seduction of Brutus; the assassination and its concomitants; and the vengeance of Antony in which his rise and Octavius' are contrasted with the decline and fall of Brutus and Cassius.[31]

Approaching the play from the position of a working director, Granville-Barker, long ago, insisted on the structual integrity of the closing phase of the play, arguing forcibly against the view that the last act is sprawling or lacks coherence:

> The play is a masterpiece of Elizabethan stagecraft, and the last act, from this point of view, especially remarkable; but only by close analysis can its technical virtues be made plain. Within the powerful ease of its larger rhythm, the constant, varied ebb and flow and interplay of purpose, character and event give it richness of dramatic life, and us the sense of its lifelikeness.[32]

More recently Alexander Leggatt has added his voice in defence of the final phase:

The long anticlimax is a dangerous but legitimate device on Shakespeare's part, to remind us, as he did after the Battle of Shrewsbury, that nothing in history is ever finished. Set against this are the characters' own attempts to see shape in their lives. These too have their equivalent in the shaping of the play itself, which can suggest an open future but must find a way for its own action to end. The last scenes are full of references to closing up a circle. But the effect is not, as at the end of *Henry v*, ultimate futility; it seems rather an attempt to see order, if only an aesthetic order, in one's existence. Cassius sees it in the fact that he is dying on his birthday.[33]

Closely related to this feature, and one which functions as another unifying force, is that of destiny. Perhaps the strongest proponent of the view that Shakespeare deliberately conveys the sense of a ruling influence by some higher power is Paul N. Siegel, who claims that 'each of the Roman history plays suggests a providence at work behind human actions'.[34] His extensively developed argument is flawed by an assumption that Shakespeare's audience was uniformly naïve, and is effectively countered by the Martindales' cogent argument:

Much Elizabethan history is strongly providentialist, or demonstrates the dangers of faction and the merits of monarchy. By contrast Shakespeare in his Roman plays seems closer to modern historical thinking in three main respects: first, because he has a strong sense that past cultures were different from present ones, together with the ability to embody that perception in the texture of his plays; secondly, because his picture of Roman history is so unidealized and so coolly secular, and involves an awareness that ethics and politics are very different pursuits; and, finally, because, as G. K. Hunter puts it, he used Plutarch to 'escape from the pressure of teleology', that is, to examine historical events which had not directly determined the present lives of his audience and which did not have to be shaped into any kind of sacred history or aetiology.[35]

Nevertheless, it is true that characters gradually acquire a sense of some powerful, ineffable force at work which ultimately determines the outcome of events. Even Plutarch gives expression to this feeling on one occasion and certainly characters in the play do so, especially when the outlook is bleak. The outstanding example is Cassius' utterance:

You know that I held Epicurus strong,
And his opinion; now I change my mind,

And partly credit things that do presage.
Coming from Sardis, on our former ensign
Two mighty eagles fell, and there they perch'd,
Gorging and feeding from our soldiers' hands,
Who to Philippi here consorted us.
This morning are they fled away and gone,
And in their steads do ravens, crows, and kites
Fly o'er our heads, and downward look on us,
As we were sickly prey; their shadows seem
A canopy most fatal, under which
Our army lies, ready to give up the ghost.

(v.i.77–89)

However, Cassius recognises the irrationality of his feelings when pressed
by Messala, concluding with an adherence to that great and overriding
Roman principle, constancy:

Mes.   Believe not so.
Cas.   I but believe it partly,
         For I am fresh of spirit, and resolv'd
         To meet all perils very constantly.

(v.i.90–2)

Rather than fate governing events, what we see is that human tendency,
in any crisis, to feel that there is some intangible force at work. Here there
is a unity between the personal and the great sweep of history. At one level
men are conscious of themselves and each other as ordinary human beings
with all kinds of idiosyncrasies and foibles; at another level they see themselves and each other as representatives of political forces, as figures on the
stage of history. This double reality or double vision is an integral part of
Julius Caesar and adds to its peculiar fascination.

What emerges from the briefest glance at some of the most significant
contributions to the discussion of genre and the unity of the play is that
unless it is seen simply as a revenge tragedy it constitutes a pathbreaking
drama which differs quite markedly from the English histories that precede
it and the tragedies which come later. Whereas in *Titus Andronicus*
Shakespeare conveys a genuine sense of a Roman world, the play itself
looks in two directions: towards the later Roman plays and towards *King
Lear*. With *Julius Caesar*, Shakespeare comes face to face with Rome for the
second time in his dramatic career, but is influenced for the first time by
Plutarch. Here he creates a truly palpable sense of Rome with its great

historical figures populating the social and physical landscape, speaking in a distinctive manner, and struggling with tensions arising from those most deep-rooted of human emotions – love, jealousy and ambition – while trying to live up to the conception of a true Roman. Entering the theatre we are drawn into a political maelstrom. We are never allowed to forget the nature of political conflict and even in the final moments there is an acute consciousness of an embryonic conflict between Antony and Octavius with the latter stealing the initiative. As Brutus makes his confident prediction about the verdict of history, the audience is provoked into a contemplation of the historical events and interpretations. There is also an attempt to assess personal and political motives, decisions and consequences – matters quite absent at the end of a tragedy.

If the question of genre had troubled the minds of Shakespeare's audience, they would probably have felt that it was a Roman play and that it was a tragedy. Its strain of revenge tragedy would almost certainly have struck a chord. But it is doubtful whether they would have been troubled further. Perhaps the foremost question in their minds on leaving the theatre would have been 'who was right?' – a question which many might have expected to have been answered. What they experienced was something opaque. For subsequent audiences justification of the assassination would be determined, largely, by the proclivity of the production or the nature of the social world outside the theatre. If Julius Caesar is identified with fascist dictators, sympathy for Brutus is strong. If the proscription scene is cut and a charismatic actor plays Antony, he can emerge as the hero. How the play is received will depend greatly on the weighting of the major protagonists and/or by a variety of directorial decisions, because it is not possible to make unequivocal statements based on the text. Moreover, even in the case of a most carefully balanced production working with an uncut text, reaction will inevitably be influenced by personal and political prejudices.

Shakespeare presents us with an enigma in such a way as to make unequivocal judgement impossible. We cannot even be certain about the kind of play it is, other than by calling it a Roman play. It is almost half a century since John Palmer[36] drew attention to a crucial unifying feature, that ubiquitous Roman character, the Roman crowd, present from the outset and playing a vital part in the determination of events. The very Romanness of *Julius Caesar* provides its chief unifying element. There is no doubt that the latter part of the play can seem sprawling or anti-climactic, but it is also possible to sustain the dramatic tension right up to the final curtain – and beyond. As the final battle ends the embryo of a future struggle emerges in the exchanges between the vividly contrasting personalities of Antony and Octavius. Already the Roman world is experiencing a process of metamorphosis. Concern is not just with the dead, but with the living, and with the process of history itself, and how that strange feeling of historical inevitability works its spell on all observers, even after we have watched, in minute detail, the interplay between personalities, values, decisions and events. The unity of the play resides in its living, pulsating Roman world and in its stimulation of that insatiable human curiosity about history – and how it might have been.

· 3 ·

Shakespeare and Plutarch:
Characters and Events in
History and Drama

Exploration of the relationship between Shakespeare's plays and his source material is invariably illuminating. In the case of the 'collaboration' between Shakespeare and Plutarch, however, analysis of the absorption and transformation of the historical material by the dramatist is enormously enriching both in terms of characterisation and in the shaping of the play. As James R. Siemon comments:

> nowhere is the debt of Shakespearean drama to historical sources more pronounced than in *Julius Caesar*. Character, incident, imagery, even entire speeches are taken, sometimes verbatim, from North's Plutarch and incorporated into the play. More interesting than the mere fact of this borrowing, however, is the way Shakespeare's play and Plutarch's history demonstrate a *shared concern not only for their subject but for the interpretation of it* [my emphasis] . . . the *Lives* create the *effect* of history by the way in which the text repeatedly interrupts its progress and violates its nascent patterns with reminders of discrepant, and even contradictory, reports among various sources. . . . Neither event nor person nor thing comes to one securely fixed into one pattern. Instead, the text urges sifting and evaluation in a way and to a degree quite foreign to the mythic.[1]

One of the most notable features of Shakespeare's use of his source material in *Julius Caesar* is the way in which he conflates events. This process begins in the opening scene where the dramatist combines Caesar's triumph over Pompey's sons (October 45 BC) with the feast of Lupercal (15 February 44 BC). Among other things this conjunction points out the incongruity between a celebration of the founding of Rome and the triumph of one great Roman general over the sons of an equally revered Roman. In the midst of these celebrations comes the warning from a soothsayer – an event which, according to Plutarch, occurred much earlier. Furthermore, a month elapsed between Cassius' first suggestion to Brutus that he join the conspiracy and the evening preceding the assassination. In the play there is a feeling of headlong pace. Even more significant is the way in which the dramatist conflates events following the assassination. According to Plutarch, Brutus made his first speech in the Capitol 'to winne the favor of the people, and to justify that they had done'.[2] On the following day he made a second speech in the market-place which was not successful. Two days after the assassination the matter was discussed in the Capitol, and Cicero's suggestion, that the conspirators be awarded honours but that Caesar's edicts should stand and that he receive the appropriate praises, was supported by Antony. Brutus acceded to Antony's request to supervise the funeral arrangements, thereby enabling him to incite the crowd against the conspirators. Shakespeare concentrates these events into the meeting between Antony and the assassins immediately after Caesar's death and the Forum scene.

The dramatist omits, totally, the historical breach between Antony and Octavius which began with antagonistic manoeuvring and culminated in a battle which Antony lost. Historically the event which inspired the proscription scene occurred several months after the assassination. Shakespeare's brief but chilling scene encapsulates a negotiation which lasted for three days and took place on the Isle of Pharos. Finally, the three weeks which separated the battles at Philippi are conflated into a single day. Hence Plutarch's recorded events, extending over a period of three years, between October 45 BC and October 42 BC, are, in the play, powerfully concentrated into a brief but indefinite time scheme. Apart from a time lapse between the fleeing of Brutus and Cassius from Rome and their meeting at Sardis, the feeling is one of a continuous and rapid unfolding of events seeming to take place in a matter of days.

Shakespeare's inventions of Calphurnia's sterility and Caesar's deafness are significant. When Caesar reminds Antony to touch Calphurnia in the chase it may be the first glimpse of his new-found superstition emphasised later by Cassius (II.i.195). Caesar's deafness in one ear brings a rich vein of irony to the moment when he asserts his super-human invulnerability. Here the dramatist points out a disjunction between reality and Caesar's cultivated public persona. Cassius' wonderfully malicious description of his role in rescuing the physically vulnerable Caesar from the Tiber is also Shakespeare's invention – an invention which is telling, given Plutarch's description of Caesar's escape from the Egyptians in Alexandria by means of his strong swimming (supporting precious books on his head!). Furthermore, the ceremonial bathing in Caesar's blood after the assassination has no counterpart in Plutarch. Likewise, there is no historical basis for the meeting of the adversaries before the battle of Philippi. This scene enables Shakespeare to develop personality contrasts and conflicts and serves as a reminder to the audience that had Cassius' will prevailed over that of Brutus, Mark Antony would not be standing there. Even more significantly, Plutarch's description of a dispute between Brutus and Cassius over who should lead the more prestigious right flank at Philippi is transferred to Octavius and Antony in the play. This brief conflict brings out the stubborn assertiveness of young Octavius, providing in embryo a rivalry which will blossom into contention for domination of the Empire in *Antony and Cleopatra*.

CHARACTERISATION

Julius Caesar

Caesar emerges from the pages of Plutarch as a man who is affable, courteous, generous, magnanimous, calculating and ambitious. As an orator he is ranked second only to Cicero, and Plutarch goes on to describe how this talent, with other attributes, served his political aspirations. Caesar's physical courage was impressive but was seen as part of his quest for honour. However, his determination to overcome disabilities, including epilepsy, was so remarkable that it won him widespread admiration. When describing Caesar's charismatic military leadership, the historian is unequivocal: 'he was so entirely beloved of his souldiers, that to doe him service . . . if Caesars honor were touched, they were invincible.'[3] Noting that Caesar had long anticipated a battle for primacy with Pompey, the historian describes how Caesar outmanoeuvred his former associate both politically and militarily. Caesar's final battle, fought in Spain, was against Pompey's sons. Plutarch records, with considerable emotion, the hostility which Caesar aroused by celebrating this victory in Rome (an emotion which is conveyed powerfully in Shakespeare's opening scene of the play):

the triumphe he made into Rome . . . did as much offend the Romanes, and more, then any thing that ever he had done before: bicause he had not overcome Captaines that were straungers, nor barbarous kinges, but had destroyed the sonnes of the noblest man in Rome, whom fortune had overthrowen. And bicause he had plucked up his race by the rootes, men did not thinke it meete for him to triumphe so.

Despite the offence caused by this triumph, Plutarch continues, the Romans appointed him perpetual Dictator, which 'was a plaine tyranny: for to this absolute power of Dictator, they added this, never to be affraied to be deposed'. Although Plutarch expresses distaste for the title and other honours that were bestowed on him, he declares that Caesar conducted himself with admirable restraint – pardoning former enemies and even elevating some to high office, including Cassius and Brutus.

Within the compass of a few pages the historian gives Shakespeare a great deal of valuable material for the first two scenes of the play. First he points to the main reason for the antagonism which Caesar attracted: 'the chiefest cause that made him mortally hated, was the covetous desire he had to be called king: which first gave the people just cause, and next his secret enemies, honest colour to beare him ill will.' Plutarch goes on to narrate events which suggest Caesar coveted the title of king, but that he wanted to test public reaction before revealing his ambition. On his return to Rome, he rebuked those who called him king when he perceived that the people were offended by the title. Moreover, at the feast of Lupercal, Antony presented Caesar with a 'Diadeame wreathed about with laurell', which brought forth a cry of approval and rejoicing, but 'not very great' and 'done onely by a few, appointed for the purpose'. When Caesar rejected the crown (twice as opposed to Shakespeare's thrice), 'then all the people together made an outcrie of joy'. The historian makes it clear, therefore, that this is no whim of Antony's but a rehearsed scheme to make another test of public opinion. Shakespeare conveys this in a much more interesting way. In a few strokes he heightens the whole scene, providing a vivid portrait of Casca, who dramatises the incident while playing the part of the cynically detached observer.

There is a fairly flat account of how the tribunes Marullus and Flavius imprisoned those who 'first saluted Caesar as king' and later removed the 'Diadeames' from Caesar's images. For these actions they were deprived of their tribuneships. Shakespeare's handling of this incident is instructive. In the opening scene he uses Marullus and Flavius to demonstrate political opposition to Caesar and to reveal the naïvety and susceptibility of the common people. In the following scene Casca, by way of a footnote to his description of Caesar's rejection of the crown, adds 'Marullus and Flavius, for pulling scarfs off Caesar's images, are put to silence' (I.ii.282–3). This terse and ambiguous comment strikes an ominous note: political opponents are quickly removed – and killed? What does 'put to silence' mean? A modern audience would probably interpret this comment as meaning 'put to death'. It may be that Shakespeare intended this interpretation, but it is more likely that he deliberately used an ambiguous expression to keep the audience wondering about the precise nature of Caesar's power and aspirations. There is certainly no ambiguity in his source: these men are simply deprived of office (though this in itself reveals Caesar's impatience with opponents and his determination to effect his will).

Shakespeare uses numerous details of the 'straunge and wonderfull signes that were sayd to be seene before Caesars death': the flames which sprang forth from the slave's hand; the noises in the night; Calphurnia's dream, who 'untill that time, was never geven to any feare or supersticion'; Caesar's sacrifice of a beast that had no heart. Furthermore, even as Caesar is about to enter the Senate-house the Soothsayer responds to his flippant comment 'The Ides of March be come' with the caution 'but yet are they not past'.

The arguments put forward by Decius Brutus, including the interpretation of Calphurnia's dream, are all taken up by Shakespeare. Caesar had such confidence in this man, Plutarch comments, that 'in his last will and testament he had appointed him to be his next [second] heire' (Octavius being the first). Artemidorus, having gained knowledge of the conspiracy, attempted to impart it to Caesar. He handed Caesar the warning with the words 'reade this memoriall to your selfe, and that quickely, for they be matters of great waight and touche you neerely'. The dramatist comes close to using this very expression, but whereas the historian adds: 'Caesar tooke it of him, but coulde never reade it, though he many times attempted it, for the number of people that did salute him', Shakespeare's Caesar takes advantage of the occasion to exhibit his commitment to the primacy of public duty over private interest: 'What touches us ourself shall be last serv'd' (III.i.8).

At this point Plutarch makes an interesting interpolation. Whereas he is generally detached when recording events, attempting to provide a clear statement of the relevant details and circumstances (citing alternative accounts where conflicting descriptions have been advanced), here he writes as a fatalist. He states that Artemidorus tried hard to give the memorial to Caesar but was prevented by the surge of the crowd, even though he continued to follow the procession. Taking this and subsequent events together, Plutarch concludes:

For these things, they may seeme to come by chaunce: but the place where the murther was prepared, and where the Senate were assembled, and where also there stoode up an image of Pompey dedicated by him selfe amongest other ornamentes which he gave unto the Theater: all these were manifest proofes that it was the ordinaunce of some god, that made this treason to be executed, specially in that verie place. It is also reported, that Cassius (though otherwise he did favour the doctrine of Epicurus) beholding the image of Pompey, before they entred into the action of their traiterous enterprise: he did softely call upon it, to aide him.

This last comment clearly fired Shakespeare's imagination: there are ten references to Pompey in the play, three of which occur within two dozen lines (i.iii.126–52). Plutarch also makes an obscure observation about Cassius suddenly breaking into 'a furious passion, and made him like a man halfe besides him selfe'. The dramatist makes sense of this incident by showing Cassius panic when he believes that Caesar is being warned of the plot.

Shakespeare uses Plutarch's brief description of the contrived pleas on behalf of Publius Cimber, but creates for Caesar a speech suggesting he has fallen victim to the self-image of the great man. Then the dramatist gives Caesar a telling little comment of which there is no hint in the source. Insisting on the futility of pleading he says: 'Doth not Brutus bootless kneel?' (iii.i.75). If Shakespeare accords Brutus a special position at this point, Plutarch provides justification for this view a little later, when he describes how Caesar fiercely resisted the assassins until he was confronted by Brutus. The picture of the assassination created by Plutarch is vivid, revealing Caesar's courage, the ensuing chaos and the way in which the assassins unintentionally wounded one another:

They . . . that had conspired his death, compassed him in on everie side with their swordes drawen in their handes, that Caesar turned him no where, but he was striken at by some, and still had naked swords in his face, and *was hacked and mangeled amonge them, as a wilde beaste taken of hunters* [my emphasis]. For it was agreed among them, that every man should geve him a wound, bicause all their partes should be in this murther: and then Brutus him selfe gave him one wounde about his privities. Men reporte also, that Caesar did still defende him selfe against the rest, running everie waye with his bodie: but when he sawe Brutus with his sworde drawen in his hande, then he pulled his gowne over his heade, and made no more resistaunce, and was driven either casually, or purposedly, by the counsell of the conspirators, against the base whereupon Pompeys image stoode, which ranne all of a goare bloude, till he was slaine. Thus it seemed, that the image tooke just revenge of Pompeys enemie, being throwen downe on the ground at his feete, and yelding up his ghost there.[4]

Caesar's response on recognising Brutus as one of the assassins is given verbal expression by Shakespeare: '*Et tu, Brute?* – Then fall Caesar!' (III.i.77). Another key point picked up by the dramatist is that of the conspirators accidentally wounding each other. Mark Antony says: 'when your vile daggers/Hack'd one another in the sides of Caesar' (v.i.39–40).

Caesar's death was marked by the appearance of a comet, which remained visible for seven nights, and by other strange phenomena. But the most clear indication that the gods were offended by the murder, Plutarch states, was the apparition witnessed by Brutus.

Clearly, Plutarch's account of Caesar's personality and the events surrounding his life and death provided a great stimulus to the dramatist's imagination. His was not, however, the only influence on the consciousness of Shakespeare and his contemporaries: the merits of Caesar, the man and the hero, had been subject to historical and literary debate since the time of the assassination. The consensus of scholarly opinion is that attitudes towards the great man and the key characters closely associated with him were ambivalent. As Geoffrey Bullough expresses the matter:

By the end of the classical epoch the main features of the chief characters in the fall of the Republic were well established. Usually two aspects of each of them were contrasted. Julius Caesar appeared as a man of paradox. On the one hand there was general agreement on his martial skill, energy, eloquence, power over his legions and the plebeians; on his kindness to his friends and soldiers, his moderation in diet, his frequent clemency. On the other hand he was widely regarded as capable of great ruthlessness, a despiser of religion, lustful, guileful, above all ambitious. Opinions were divided on whether he sought the Civil War and Pompey's death, but most ancient writers agreed that inordinate ambition was his lifelong driving-force; he could not bear to be second, and he wished to rule the state, possibly as hereditary monarch, certainly as a 'tyrant' in the Greek sense of the word. Though some writers thought his murder might be justified, the majority regarded it as a wicked act. The ambivalence found in Cicero and developed by Plutarch affected the whole Caesar-tradition, and we can see later historians striving towards a balanced view which would take account of both sides of his personality and career.[5]

The great classical biographers and historians, Plutarch, Suetonius, Appian and Dio Cassius (all of them known to Shakespeare, with the possible exception of the last named), recognise the duality in Caesar's personality and strive to provide a balanced view. Plutarch carefully delineates Caesar's qualities, deficiencies and his occasional lapses of judgement, but leaves no doubt about belief in his greatness and the folly of the assassination. Nevertheless, he is also powerfully attracted by the nobility and integrity of Brutus, against whom he cites only two serious misdeeds (the assassination and the granting to his soldiers the right to sack Thessalonica and Lacedaemon if they were successful against Antony and Octavius). Suetonius extols Caesar's virtues but concludes that 'he might be thought both to have abused his soveraintie, and worthily to have been murthered'.[6] Appian is unwavering in his admiration of Caesar, but also reveals great respect for Brutus and Cassius, 'most noble and worthy Romanes, and but for one facte ever folowed vertue'. As for the motives of the other conspirators, he is noncommittal: 'eyther for enuye of his greatnesse, or for zeale of their countrey'.[7]

Of the many critics who have examined the historical responses to Caesar and his assassination, Ernest Schanzer provides what is probably the most succinct and perceptive analysis:

> Perhaps more than any other figure in history, Julius Caesar has evoked a divided response in the minds of those who have written about him. Indeed, it would not be an exaggeration to say that such a response, made up of attraction and repulsion, admiration and hostility, was the prevailing one among informed and educated men throughout Antiquity, the Middle Ages, and the Renaissance, so that we can speak of it as forming a tradition extending from Caesar's own day down to that of Shakespeare.

But he adds an important caveat: 'Where in the popular tradition Caesar was extolled and his assassins execrated, educated men, both in the Middle Ages and the Renaissance, derived from their reading of the ancients a predominantly divided response.'[8] This divided response is certainly apparent in the most celebrated of European scholars, Montaigne, and in Sir Thomas Elyot's influential book, *The Governour* (1531).

Though it is true that critics, at the polar extremes, have accused Shakespeare of caricaturing a great man or of elevating a tyrant, most have recognised a duality in the character of Caesar who exhibits greatness and arrogance, generosity of spirit and self-importance. Maurice Charney expresses the view that:

The official Caesar of Shakespeare's play is presented with all the pomp and ceremony of a great public person. Yet he is curiously undercut by our image of Caesar the private man, full of physical infirmities and an irritating insistence on his own dignity.[9]

For Mark Hunter, 'the personality of Julius moves before us as something right royal'; though 'not indeed immune from calumnious stroke'.[10] While for John Palmer: 'The essential greatness of Caesar being thus assumed, Shakespeare is free to exhibit in him human weaknesses apparently inconsistent with it.'[11] It is as if Shakespeare presents Caesar as a victim of his own achievements and undoubted greatness. He comes to believe in the deification which is taking place around him. This process can be seen at work in Caesar's first entrance. Surrounded by a great crowd, he utters only one word before Casca calls for silence. Antony addresses Caesar as 'my lord' and in response to his master's request replies ingratiatingly: 'When Caesar says, "Do this," it is perform'd' (i.ii.10). As soon as the Soothsayer calls on Caesar, Casca demands silence once more. The power of his name already apparent, Caesar refers to himself in the third person. Within the compass of twenty-four lines the audience is made aware of the grandeur of Caesar and the potentially corrupting effect of subservience and adulation. Caesar's response to the Soothsayer also implies belief in the infallibility of his intuitive powers. This is wonderfully ironic in a play where judgements are continually flawed. There is no questioning, no wariness, just a brief look followed by confident assessment.

Even after Caesar has left the stage, adulation of the great man is indicated by the shouts that make Brutus so anxious about 'some new honours that are heap'd on Caesar' (i.ii.132). But when he returns the atmosphere has changed: there is discomfort and embarrassment, and Caesar seems more disposed to be wary – but not for long. No sooner has he made a penetrating appraisal of Cassius than he refuses to make use of it:

I rather tell thee what is to be fear'd
Than what I fear; for always I am Caesar.

But the confident assertion is immediately followed by the intimately human comment that underlines his vulnerability:

Come on my right hand, for this ear is deaf,
(i.ii.208–10)

Caesar then leaves the stage to the accompaniment of music, only to be the subject of mockery by Casca – the very character who was first to demand silence for 'Caesar'. Audience response to Caesar's first scene, therefore, is one of ambivalence. There is a sense of the character's greatness but this is undercut by a sense of incongruity. The adulation is willingly accepted by Caesar; he underestimates the antagonism he generates and his own vulnerability. Hailed in public, he is denigrated behind his back, and this process itself generates a mixture of contempt and sympathy.

Caesar's next appearance (II.ii) is even more marked by a determination to disregard dangers by reference to his invulnerability. In response to Calphurnia's pleading, Caesar is foolishly assertive:

Caesar shall go forth. The things that threaten'd me
Ne'er look'd but on my back; when they shall see
The face of Caesar, they are vanished.
(II.ii.10–12)

When the augurers lend support to the desperate Calphurnia, Caesar, preferring to believe in his potent self-image, comes to his own conclusion:

The gods do this in shame of cowardice:
Caesar should be a beast without a heart
If he should stay at home to-day for fear.
No, Caesar shall not. Danger knows full well
That Caesar is more dangerous than he.
We are two lions litter'd in one day,
And I the elder and more terrible,
And Caesar shall go forth.
(II.ii.41–8)

Caesar's use of imagery is instructive. If Brutus' imagery gets in the way of clear reasoning in his orchard soliloquy, here imagery is characterised by extravagance and absurdity. In striving to make himself more than human, Caesar is ridiculous. Moreover, this posturing is punctured when he changes his mind in response to Calphurnia's pleading (on her knees). The co-mingling of man and myth is apparent in the dialogue between Caesar and Calphurnia. Indeed, the husband–wife relationships constitute one of the powerful contrasts in the play. Whereas Granville-Barker sees Calphurnia as 'a nervous, fear-haunted creature ... isolated and tremulous',[12] the Brutus–Portia relationship reminds us, as G. Wilson Knight observes, 'of Hotspur and Lady Percy'.[13] Portia's death and the suffering it causes Brutus lie at the heart of the quarrel scene. It is as if the vital spark in Brutus is extinguished after the death of Portia. There is a sense of an external effort which is quite unsupported by inner vitality. Significantly, no more is heard of Calphurnia after her scene. Caesar may seem a little patronising but we are back with the man beneath the image. There is a tenderness in the lines,

> Mark Antony shall say I am not well,
> And for thy humour I will stay at home.
> Here's Decius Brutus; he shall tell them so.
>   (II.ii.55–7)

Within seconds, however, the tetchy, irrational, self-conscious Caesar is adopting a stance, scorning the idea of telling a lie – the very lie he proposed himself! In response to Decius' 'I come to fetch you to the Senate House', the grand manner is quickly assumed:

> *Caes.* And you are come in very happy time
>   To bear my greeting to the senators,
>   And tell them that I will not come to-day:
>   Cannot, is false; and that I dare not, falser;
>   I will not come to-day. Tell them so, Decius.
> *Cal.* Say he is sick.
> *Caes.*   Shall Caesar send a lie?
>   Have I in conquest stretch'd mine arm so far,
>   To be afeared to tell greybeards the truth?
>   Decius, go tell them Caesar will not come.
>   (II.ii.59–68)

When Decius then seeks a reason to communicate to the Senate, Caesar is emphatic: 'The cause is in my will: I will not come' (II.ii.71). Yet the man who prides himself on being 'constant as the northern star' (III.i.60) reverses his decision as soon as Decius reinterprets Calphurnia's dream and follows up with a mixture of seduction (promise of further honours) and threat (exposure to ridicule):

>   The Senate have concluded
>   To give this day a crown to mighty Caesar.
>   If you shall send them word you will not come,
>   Their minds may change. Besides, it were a mock
>   Apt to be render'd, for some one to say,
>   'Break up the Senate till another time,

When Caesar's wife shall meet with better dreams.'
If Caesar hide himself, shall they not whisper,
'Lo, Caesar is afraid'?

                                        (ii.ii.93–101)

Just when Caesar, by exhibiting both egotism and naïvety, has fallen in the
esteem of the audience, the other Caesar once more emerges – affable,
relaxed, welcoming and warm-hearted. The last part of the dialogue is
telling:

Caes.	Bid them prepare within.
	I am to blame to be thus waited for.
	Now, Cinna; now, Metellus; what, Trebonius:
	I have an hour's talk in store for you;
	Remember that you call on me to-day:
	Be near me, that I may remember you.
Treb.	Caesar, I will: [*Aside.*] And so near will I be,
	That your best friends shall wish I had been further.
Caes.	Good friends, go in, and taste some wine with me;
	And we, like friends, will straightway go together.
Bru.	[*Aside.*] That every like is not the same, O Caesar!
	The heart of Brutus earns to think upon.

                                        (ii.ii.118–29)

Trebonius' aside is so distasteful that audience sympathy immediately
moves back to Caesar. Commentators have noted an echo of the Last
Supper, but if Brutus is cast as the Judas his aside compels compassion. For
here is a man suffering acute anguish and feeling the falsity of this position.
    There is yet a further counter-movement in the flow of audience
sympathy as Caesar adopts the posture of public servant when rejecting
Artemidorus' suit: 'What touches us ourself shall be last serv'd' (iii.i.8),
and moments later when he rejects the plea on behalf of Publius Cimber:

              I must prevent thee, Cimber.
These couchings and these lowly courtesies
Might fire the blood of ordinary men,
And turn pre-ordinance and first decree
Into the law of children. Be not fond,
To think that Caesar bears such rebel blood
That will be thaw'd from the true quality
With that which melteth fools – I mean sweet words,

Low-crooked curtsies, and base spaniel fawning.
Thy brother by decree is banished:
If thou dost bend and pray and fawn for him,
I spurn thee like a cur out of my way.
Know, Caesar doth not wrong, nor without cause
Will he be satisfied.

(III.i.35–48)

The last phrase is particularly telling bearing in mind earlier comments on the likelihood that the original construction was 'Caesar did never wrong, but with just cause', which sums up precisely the state of mind of the infallible ruler. And there is still further alienation of sympathy when Caesar elaborates his vision of himself as the constant star – and, therefore, the only true Roman:

I could be well mov'd, if I were as you;
If I could pray to move, prayers would move me;
But I am constant as the northern star,
Of whose true-fix'd and resting quality
There is no fellow in the firmament.
The skies are painted with unnumber'd sparks,
They are all fire, and every one doth shine;
But there's but one in all doth hold his place.
So in the world: 'tis furnish'd well with men,
And men are flesh and blood, and apprehensive;
Yet in the number I do know but one
That unassailable holds on his rank,
Unshak'd of motion; and that I am he,
Let me a little show it, even in this,
That I was constant Cimber should be banish'd
And constant do remain to keep him so.

(III.i.58–73)

Dowden has remarked perceptively that: 'The real man Caesar disappears for himself under the greatness of the Caesar myth. He forgets himself as he actually is, and knows only the vast legendary power named Caesar.'[14] Only the bloody act of murder can reverse the flow of sympathy in Caesar's direction.

What Shakespeare achieves in the scenes with Caesar is an astonishing movement of sympathy away from and towards this great figure. The audience enter the theatre *knowing* that they are going to see a great man walk out of history on to the stage, but once in the theatre they are never allowed a settled judgement: they encounter a man possessed of vigour, greatness and, to use the medieval term, gentilesse; but they also perceive decline in the form of physical debility, egotism and grandiloquence. It is the dynamic tension with which these elements are held together that makes for such telling characterisation.

Brutus and Cassius

Plutarch's *Life of Brutus* begins by noting that Marcus Brutus was a descendant of Junius Brutus, in whose honour a statue was set up because of the courage he displayed in driving out the Tarquins, the last kings of Rome. However, the historian promptly contrasts the two personalities: Junius was so severe that he ordered the execution of his own sons; Marcus Brutus, on the other hand, 'framed his manners of life by the rules of vertue and studie of Philosophie'. Brutus' mentor was his uncle Marcus Cato, whose daughter, Portia, he married. The historian describes Brutus' mastery of Latin and his qualities as an orator, going on to illustrate his favoured style of Greek oratory – a style which Shakespeare unmistakably adopts for Brutus' Forum speech. Very early on in his account of Brutus' character and life, Plutarch mentions an event which must have startled and impressed the dramatist. He states that when Caesar and Pompey took up arms against each other, it was presumed that Brutus would side with Caesar because Pompey had executed Brutus' father. And indeed, prior to this conflict, Brutus would not deign to speak to Pompey. However, 'Brutus preferring the respect of his contrie and common wealth, before private affection, and perswading himselfe that Pompey had juster cause to enter into armes then Caesar: he then tooke parte with Pompey.' Here we have, in essence, the character of the man who could conspire the assassination of his benefactor for the good of his country, and who, in Shakespeare's play, tells Antony that were he Caesar's son he would be satisfied that the assassination was justified. The source of this breathtaking naïvety is surely to be found in Plutarch's description of the man who joins forces with his father's murderer for what he believes is the good of his country.

The historian then embarks on a fascinating discussion of the triangular relationships between Caesar, Brutus and Cassius. The latter two were linked through marriage – Brutus' sister Junia was the wife of Cassius. However, they fell out while contesting the Praetorshippe, the position of chief judge of the city. Caesar, though he felt that Cassius was the more deserving on account of his military exploits, appointed Brutus to the post. Plutarch explores all the possibilities for Caesar's preference, including such cynical interpretations as the desire to promote conflict between

Cassius and Brutus or because he feared Brutus' 'great minde, authority, and frends'. Cassius, in cautioning Brutus against Caesar, gave neither of these reasons, but 'sayd Caesar gave him, not to honor his vertue, but to weaken his constant minde, framing it to the bent of his bowe'. Caesar, Plutarch suggests, was wary of Brutus, so that he 'did not trust him overmuch', but 'he trusted his good nature, and fayer condicions'. When cautioned by friends against Antony and Dolabella, Caesar 'aunswered, that these fat long heared men made him not affrayed, but the leane and whitely faced fellowes, meaning that, by Brutus and Cassius'. It would appear from Plutarch's account that Caesar realised he could not depend on Brutus' unqualified support, but that he thought him incapable of duplicity. Caesar also felt that the long-term political interests of Brutus would deter him from serious opposition. However, 'Cassius being a chollericke man, and hating Caesar privatlie, more then he did the tyrannie openlie: he incensed Brutus against him.' The historian enumerates various personal reasons for Cassius' antagonism towards Caesar, but also gives him credit for strong political conviction: 'For Cassius even from his cradell could not abide any maner of tyrans.' Shakespeare attached little importance to this comment: the Cassius of the play is a passionate man for whom personal considerations are of overriding importance.

Plutarch gives a clear indication of the widespread discontent caused by Caesar's behaviour, and the perceived threat he represented to political freedoms and traditions. There were genuine appeals to Brutus to redress these wrongs: 'But for Brutus, his frendes and contrie men, both by divers procurementes, and sundrie rumors of the citie, and by many bills also, did openlie call and procure him to doe that he did.' In the play these appeals are forged by Cassius and his associates in order to convince Brutus of the groundswell of opposition to Caesar and, more importantly, to persuade him that his fellow citizens look to him as the supreme defender of freedom. Both historian and dramatist emphasise the strategic role of Brutus: his reputation as a man of integrity was essential to the conspirators' political credibility. The historian provides some deft touches in his account of the development of the conspiracy. Cicero was not invited to join them because 'they were affrayed that he being a coward by nature, and age also having increased his feare, he woulde quite turne and alter all their purpose, and quenche the heate of their enterprise'. In the play, it is Brutus who rejects the proposal that Cicero be invited to participate – on the grounds that he would automatically assume the leadership. Ironically, Brutus immediately takes command and makes a number of vital decisions – all of which are wrong. Plutarch writes admiringly of the conspirators' remarkable confidence in each other, disdaining to undertake an oath of secrecy. Such an oath-taking is proposed in the play but Brutus rather self-righteously dismisses the idea. The historian makes a sharp contrast between Brutus' ability to appear perfectly natural and unperturbed in public while being racked with anxiety at home. This perturbation, however, does not arise from doubts about the justice of the act but from the 'daungers that might happen'. Shakespeare's Brutus is concerned exclusively with the morality of the action. Indeed, his fellow conspirators barely look beyond the assassination, and when they do (by proposing that Antony be killed along with Caesar) Brutus exercises a veto.

Plutarch is unequivocal in stating that Brutus was alone in opposing the killing of Antony. The reasons advanced by the conspirators for killing Antony were: first, he was 'a wicked man' who favoured tyranny; secondly, he held great sway with the soldiers; thirdly, he was daring and by virtue of holding the office of Consul had considerable influence. These were reasons enough for considering Antony a potentially dangerous adversary. Brutus, however, argued that it was 'not honest' and that there was hope of reform in Antony, who, on the death of Caesar, 'would willingly helpe his contry to recover her libertie'. Initially, Antony did indeed play the role of peacemaker. However, just when everything seemed to have been resolved, Antony moved that Caesar's will be 'red openly' and that he be buried honourably. 'Cassius stowtly spake against it. But Brutus went with the motion, and agreed unto it', and this, Plutarch states, was Brutus' 'second fault' (the first being his opposition to the killing of Antony). When the people learned that they were the recipients of 75 drachmas each and had been bequeathed gardens and arbours they 'loved him, and were marvelous sory for him'. Having set the stage, Antony walked on to it:

> Afterwards when Caesars body was brought into the market place, Antonius making his funerall oration in praise of the dead, according to the auncient custom of Rome, and perceiving that his wordes moved the common people to compassion: he framed his eloquence to make their harts yerne the more, and taking Caesars gowne all bloudy in his hand, he layed it open to the sight of them all, shewing what a number of cuts and holes it had upon it. Therewithall the people fell presently into such a rage and mutinie, that there was no more order kept amongest the common people.

From this brief but suggestive comment, Shakespeare draws inspiration for Antony's powerful oration. Plutarch does not indicate whether Antony had been playing a waiting game or had merely acted in response to propitious circumstances, whereas Shakespeare leaves no doubt about Antony's calculation. Plutarch makes it plain that when their houses were attacked 'the conspirators forseeing the daunger before, had wisely provided for them selves, and fled'. Brutus was alone in failing to foresee the outcome. These critical miscalculations by Brutus form a structural feature of the play.

The substance of the scene in which Portia pleads with Brutus to open his heart to her is furnished by Plutarch. On the day of the assassination Portia, despite her resolution, was so overcome by anxiety that she collapsed and was taken to bed. When Brutus received the news, 'it grieved him, as it is to be presupposed: yet he left not of the care of his contrie and common wealth, neither went home to his house for any news he heard'. Indeed, Brutus retained the presence of mind to calm his associates with a look when they were on the brink of panic believing momentarily that the conspiracy was being exposed. Describing the assassination, the historian emphasises Caesar's desperate fight to escape his assailants until he saw Brutus 'with a sworde drawen in his hande readie to strike at him: then he let Cascaes hande goe, and casting his gowne over his face, suffered everie man to strike at him that woulde'. This sentence, along with the account of Caesar's concern for Brutus' safety at Pharsalia, his pardon and Caesar's subsequent generosity, constitutes the only evidence of a special relationship between the two men. Plutarch never writes of them embracing or working closely together. Thus there is something enigmatic about the Caesar–Brutus relationship both in Plutarch's narrative and in the play.

The riot following Antony's Forum speech and Caesar's cremation resulted in the strange murder of Cinna who was mistaken for his namesake – one of the assassins. This Cinna was a friend of Caesar's who left his sick-bed to attend the funeral after experiencing a dream in which Caesar led him to supper against his will. The incident evidently fired Shakespeare's imagination, because he created out of it a chilling scene consisting of an amalgam of tragedy and farce. It is this incident which persuaded Brutus and Cassius to flee from Rome 'within a fewe dayes after'. Brutus and Cassius fled to Antium and waited for the pendulum to swing their way again, being conscious, as Plutarch puts it, of the 'fickle and unconstant' nature of the 'multitude'. Indeed, this change of attitude did occur because of Antony's arrogant and dictatorial behaviour, but Brutus, fearing the presence of Caesar's soldiers who might seek revenge, did not return to Rome. Thus into the vacuum stepped the young Octavius, 'the sonne of Julius Caesars nece, whome he had adopted for his sonne, and made his heire, by his last will and testament'. Antony, initially underestimating this young man, attempted to push him aside when he arrived in Rome but Octavius soon began 'to curry favor with the common people'.

He 'tooke upon him his adopted fathers name, and made distribution amonge them of the money which his father had bequeathed unto them'. By a variety of stratagems Octavius outmanoeuvred Antony and drove him out of Italy. The rejoicing was shortlived, however, for Octavius maintained an army and sued for Consul although it was contrary to law. When the Senate turned to Brutus for salvation, Octavius made overtures to Antony. Although he was only twenty years old, Octavius was made Consul. He soon appointed judges to condemn and sentence Brutus and Cassius. Moving with speed and ruthless efficiency, Octavius Caesar divided the Empire between Antony, Lepidus and himself. The triumvirate then 'set up billes of proscription and outlawry, condemning two hundred of the noblest men of Rome to suffer death, and among that number, Cicero was one'.

In response to developments in Rome, Brutus and Cassius each gathered an army and joined forces in Smyrna – an achievement which Plutarch describes with admiration. Though the circumstances of their meeting were propitious they soon fell to quarrelling. Plutarch prefaces his account of the dispute with character portraits:

> And men reputed [Cassius] commonly to be very skilfull in warres, but otherwise marvelous chollerick and cruell, who sought to rule men by feare, rather then with lenitie: and on the other side he was too familiar with his friends, and would jest too brodely with them. But Brutus in contrary manner, for his vertue and valliantnes, was well-beloved of the people and his owne, esteemed of noble men, and hated of no man, not so much as of his enemies: bicause he was a marvelous lowly and gentle person, noble minded, and would never be in any rage, nor caried away with pleasure and covetousnes, but had ever an upright mind with him, and would never yeeld to any wronge or injustice, the which was the chiefest cause of his fame, of his rising, and of the good will that every man bare him: for they were all perswaded that his intent was good . . . as for Cassius, a hot, chollerick and cruell man, that would oftentymes be caried away from justice for gayne: it was certainly thought that he made warre, and put him selfe into sundry daungers, more to have absolute power and authoritie, then to defend the libertie of his contry. . . . And in contrary manner, his enemies them selves did never reprove Brutus, for any such chaunge or desire. For, it was sayd that Antonius spake it openly divers tymes, that he thought, that of all them that had slayne Caesar, there was none but Brutus only that was moved to doe it as thinking the acte commendable of it selfe: but that all the other conspirators did conspire his death, for some private malice or envy, that they otherwise did beare unto him.

The two quarrels between Brutus and Cassius described in Plutarch are conflated to a single event by Shakespeare but he incorporates some of the characteristics the historian ascribes to Cassius. The crucial last section forms the basis of Antony's panegyric over Brutus' body at the end of the play.

The omens turned against Brutus and Cassius the day before the battle of Philippi. The eagles that had followed them so faithfully suddenly departed, and despite the thoroughness of their spiritual observances they encountered more bad omens, disconcerting leaders and men alike. Even more demoralising for Brutus was the appearance of a strange 'image' which said: 'I am thy ill angell, Brutus, and thou shalt see me by the citie of Philippes.' This did not prevent Brutus winning the first battle, but shortly before the second battle, 'this spirit appeared again unto him, but spake never a word'.[15] The historian describes the last conflict of views between Cassius and Brutus as they contemplate the forthcoming battle:

> Cassius was of opinion not to trye this warre at one battell, but rather to delay tyme, and to drawe it out in length, considering that they were the stronger in money, and the weaker in men and armors. But Brutus in contrary manner, did alway before, and at that tyme also, desire nothing more, then to put all to the hazard of battell, as soone as might be possible: to the ende he might either quickely restore his contry to her former libertie, or rid him forthwith of this miserable world.

Plutarch goes on to describe how, over supper, Brutus engaged in lively conversation while forlorn Cassius turned to Messala, saying: 'I protest unto thee, and make thee my witnes, that I am compelled against my minde and will (as Pompey the great was) to jeopard the libertie of our contry, to the hazard of a battel.' Shakespeare uses these lines almost word for word and records another significant piece of information imparted by Plutarch – that the following day was Cassius' birthday. The sense (though not the structure nor the beauty) of the leaders' parting speech is taken from Plutarch; so too is Brutus' condemnation of Cato's suicide allied with his own determination to kill himself rather than be taken captive.

Cassius' generosity of spirit again emerged when Brutus requested the right wing of the attack. Cassius conceded this privilege even though he was the older and more experienced soldier. In the event Brutus' orders were misunderstood with the result that his attack was a hopelessly disorganised affair. Despite this disarray his force triumphed whereas Cassius' wing was defeated by Antony. Had there been a clear understanding of the situation, the day might well have belonged to Brutus and Cassius:

For nothing undid them, but that Brutus went not to helpe Cassius, thinking he had overcome them, as him selfe had done: and Cassius on the other side taried not for Brutus, thinking he had bene overthrowen, as him selfe was.

Plutarch goes on to recount how Cassius, having fled, stood on a hill attempting to discern Brutus' position: 'howebeit Cassius him selfe sawe nothing, for his sight was verie bad' (a detail picked up by Shakespeare). Titinius rode out to evaluate the situation, and was greeted by Brutus' men. Unfortunately his colleagues mistakenly believed he had been taken captive; Cassius retired to his tent with the words: 'I have lived to see one of my best frendes taken, for my sake, before my face.' He was later found with his head severed; his slave Pindarus 'was never seene more'. When Titinius realised what had happened, he blamed himself for delay and promptly killed himself. Brutus on arrival at the camp was confronted by this grim sight. Praising Cassius, he called him 'the last of all the Romanes, being unpossible that Rome should ever breede againe so noble and valiant a man as he'[16] – words closely echoed by Shakespeare. Plutarch goes on to recount how Brutus restored the morale and confidence of his men, whereas Shakespeare compacts the deaths of Cassius and Brutus. Despite a second visitation from the 'monstrous spirit' and encountering many setbacks, Brutus fought well but lost because of the cowardly behaviour of Cassius' soldiers. Brutus, Plutarch comments, 'in the middest of the conflict, did all that was possible for a skillful Captaine and valliant souldier: both for his wisedom, as also for his hardinesse, for the obtaining of victorie'. A number of small details of the battle recorded by Plutarch are taken up by Shakespeare: the courage of Marcus Cato's son who called aloud his name and that of his father; Lucilius' diversionary surrender in Brutus' name when his leader was on the brink of capture. Shakespeare also follows Plutarch closely when Lucilius addresses Antony:

> Antonius, I dare assure thee, that no enemie hath taken, nor shall take Marcus Brutus alive: and I beseech God keepe him from that fortune. For wheresoever he be found, alive or dead: he will be found like him selfe.

And Antony's response:

> I doe assure you, you have taken a better bootie, then that you followed. . . . For, I had rather have suche men my frendes, as this man here, then enemies. Then he embraced Lucilius, and at that time delivered him to one of his frendes in custodie, and Lucilius ever after served him faithfullie, even to his death.

Again Plutarch's description of Brutus seeking the aid of his friends to commit suicide is followed faithfully by Shakespeare, as is the substance of Brutus' dying words:

> Then taking every man by the hand, he sayd these words unto them with a cheerefull countenance: It rejoyceth my hart that not one of my frends hath failed me at my neede, and I do not complaine of my fortune, but only for my contries sake: for, as for me, I thinke my selfe happier than they that have overcome, considering that I leave a perpetuall fame of our corage and manhoode, the which our enemies the conquerors shall never attaine unto by force nor money, neither can let their posteritie to say, that they being naughtie and unjust men, have slaine good men, to usurpe tyrannical power not pertaining to them.

The dramatist, however, effects subtle shifts which cast an ironical light on Brutus. For the words: 'It rejoyceth my hart that not one of my frends hath failed me at my neede', Shakespeare has:

> My heart doth joy that yet in all my life
> I found no man but he was true to me.
> (v.v.34–5)

The sentence in Plutarch does not provoke any thought of Brutus' personal betrayal of Caesar; Shakespeare's lines heighten our consciousness of that betrayal – and Brutus' lack of awareness of it. Likewise, Shakespeare's lines give Brutus an abrasive, over-confident quality not present in Plutarch:

> I shall have glory by this losing day
> More than Octavius and Mark Antony
> By this vile conquest shall attain unto.
> (v.v.36–8)

This difference in tone invites the audience to reflect on historical judgements. Brutus was by no means extolled in the way he imagined: even those most favourably disposed towards him were ambivalent, whereas many authorities reviled him. One thing to emerge clearly from the play is that Brutus precipitates the very defeat of democracy that he sought to preserve. It takes Mark Antony's generous and tender words for the audience to be left with a feeling of the nobility of Brutus (v.v.68-75).

Plutarch records that some said Strato held Brutus' sword for him, and that both he and Messala gave themselves up to Octavius, who accepted their offers of service. Shakespeare follows this closely, including Strato's words on being brought before Octavius: 'Caesar, beholde, here is he that did the last service to my Brutus.' One significant difference is that the dramatist gives these events a political edge. The feeling conveyed is that Antony and Octavius do not act out of a sense of generosity or good fellowship but that they are shrewdly gathering capable and loyal men around them as a matter of self-interest. Plutarch provides an ambiguous footnote on the death of Portia, citing the opinions of earlier writers who stated that she 'tooke hotte burning coles, and cast them into her mouth, and kept her mouth so close, that she choked her selfe'. Shakespeare, of course, brings news of this sad event into the heart of the quarrel scene.

In his evaluation of Julius Caesar's exercise of authority, Plutarch comes down heavily against the justice of the assassination, asserting:

> it seemed he rather had the name and opinion onely of a tyranne, then otherwise that he was so in deede. For there never followed any tyrannicall nor cruell act, but contrarilie, it seemed that he was a mercifull Phisition, whom God had ordeyned of speciall grace to be Governor of the Empire of Rome, and to set all thinges againe at quiet stay, the which required the counsell and authoritie of an absolute Prince.

And he insists that Brutus could not escape censure for murdering his benefactor:

> the greatest reproache they could object against Brutus, was: that Julius Caesar having saved his life, and pardoned all the prisoners also taken in battell, as many as he had made request for, taking him for his frende and honoring him above all his other frends. Brutus notwithstanding had imbrued his hands in his blood.

Nevertheless, Plutarch defends Brutus on the grounds that his motives were of the highest – even his enemies agreeing that he sought only to 'restore the Empire of Rome againe, to her former state and government'. The historian also makes the point that despite the difficulties of plotting the assassination it was successfully accomplished because Brutus chose 'honest men, or else that by his choyse of them, he made them good men'. The purity of Brutus' motives is demonstrated, Plutarch claims, by the honourable burial afforded him by one of his enemies, Antony, whilst the other, Octavius, 'reserved his honors and memories of him'.[17]

Thus, though Plutarch condemns the assassination, he cannot bring himself to damn the leader of the conspiracy. Parallels can be detected in critical evaluations of Shakespeare's character, though there are pro- and anti-Brutus factions. On this critical issue Norman Sanders has made the perceptive comment that 'the puzzle of Brutus is more dramatically significant than the enigma of Caesar, for on it depends how one views the achievement of the whole play – even what kind of play one takes it to be'.[18] Perhaps the most telling phrase used in seeking to unravel the mystery of Brutus' character is Dowden's, who sees him as 'studious of self-perfection'.[19] Mark Hunter is a critic who carefully analyses Brutus' character and ultimately provides a damning judgement:

> Noble-hearted and sincere beyond question, he is intellectually dishonest. Fanatic as he is, he has never schooled himself to face facts. . . . His self-righteousness renders him incapable of recognising the possibility that he himself, in opinion or conduct, can ever be wrong.[20]

G. Wilson Knight also articulates a criticism of Brutus' character which has received widespread assent:

> He often refers to himself in a strain which repels by its egoism. . . . He is so enwrapped in a sense of his own honour that others can make no headway against his will. The conspirators always give way to him. Cassius cannot resist his self-haloed personality ever. . . . It cannot be too strongly emphasized that the conspiracy without Brutus might have been a life-force, a creating of order, not a destruction. So he ruins first Caesar, then the cause of his own party. . . . Brutus' honour pains and slays Portia, drives Cassius in their quarrel almost to madness, while Brutus remains ice-cold, armed appallingly in 'honesty'. He shows little emotion at his dear ones' death. You can do nothing with him. He is so impossibly noble: and when we forget his nobility he becomes just 'impossible'. . . . Virtue, to Brutus, is a quality to be rigidly distinguished from love. Love regularly conflicts with it.[21]

Hugh M. Richmond carries this line of argument even further, commenting: 'Brutus fails altogether to evolve during the action of the play. To the last he remains convinced, like most dogmatic moralists, that it is the perfection of the will that constitutes the consummation of all human endeavor.' He concludes: 'If there is a moral to the play, it is . . . "sincerity is not enough"'.[22] A similar conclusion has been reached by L. C. Knights, for whom 'Brutus was a man who thought that an abstract "common good" could be achieved without due regard to the complexities of the actual; a man who tried to divorce his political thinking and his political action from what he knew, and what he was, as a full human person.'[23] William and Barbara Rosen explore the character of Brutus with the aim of revealing how his moral strength is also his fundamental weakness:

> Brutus can kill Caesar to prevent tyranny, yet he cannot safeguard the deed by eliminating Antony as well, nor can he strengthen his cause by resorting to forced loans to finance his army. He will neither abdicate judgement in favor of the practical advice of Cassius nor bow to the necessary compromises of strategy and power. His moral strength is paradoxically the source of his weakness in the public world.[24]

There are highly sympathetic critical evaluations of Brutus, too, but even the most ardent supporter of Shakespeare's character would be compelled to admit a strong element of truth in most of these criticisms. What is it, then, that secures for Brutus such admiration and affection given his character defects and political ineptitude? The enigma of Shakespeare's Brutus is at least as tantalising as that of the historical personage who has perplexed and divided historians throughout the ages, and this elusiveness is apparent from the outset. Before Cassius even begins to entice him into joining the conspiracy it is clear that Brutus has been anxiously contemplating the position of Caesar. Like Caesar, adopting the mode of referring to himself in the third person, he states that 'poor Brutus' is 'with himself at war' (i.ii.45). Yet, as soon as Cassius begins to commend Brutus he is rebuffed:

> Into what dangers would you lead me, Cassius,
> That you would have me seek into myself
> For that which is not in me?
>
> (i.ii.62–4)

It is the flourish and shouting off-stage that cause Brutus to let slip his anxieties:

> What means this shouting? I do fear the people
> Choose Caesar for their king.
>
> (i.ii.78–9)

The cue encourages Cassius to bound into his 'story' with such enthusiasm that he quickly overreaches himself, letting personal animus rise above the political case he wishes to make against Caesar. Before Cassius gets into his stride, however, Brutus makes a comment which reveals his area of vulnerability, both to Cassius and to the audience:

> What is it that you would impart to me?
> If it be aught toward the general good,
> Set honour in one eye, and death i'th'other,
> And I will look on both indifferently;
> For let the gods so speed me as I love
> The name of honour more than I fear death.
>   (I.ii.83-8)

This assertion reveals a passion which transcends a statement of principle. Brutus sounds as though he longs to give that abstract quality 'honour' concrete expression. And it is difficult to determine the impact on Brutus of Cassius' catalogue of Caesar's infirmities, his wonderful iconic reference to Aeneas, and his vigorously expressed malice, because Brutus' response is to the excitement off-stage:

>   Another general shout?
> I do believe that these applauses are
> For some new honours that are heap'd on Caesar.
>   (I.ii.130-2)

Spurred on by this reaction, Cassius continues his theme, but though the vigour of the language is maintained the personal antagonism towards Caesar is now held in check. His concluding lines touch exactly the right vein:

> When could they say, till now, that talk'd of Rome,
> That her wide walks encompass'd but one man?
> Now is it Rome indeed, and room enough,
> When there is in it but one only man.
> O, you and I have heard our fathers say,
> There was a Brutus once that would have brook'd
> Th'eternal devil to keep his state in Rome
> As easily as a king.
>   (I.ii.152-9)

Brutus' response shows clearly that he is ready to be drawn into the conspiracy. Any personal feeling he has for Caesar is nothing compared with his desire to prove himself a true 'son of Rome'.

The following sequence is telling, for when Caesar appears with his 'chidden train' (i.ii.182), unlike his historical counterpart he makes no reference to Brutus. He detects Cassius' antagonism but sees nothing of Brutus' passion or resentment. This question of personal evaluation is central to the play because all the major characters 'interpret' themselves and others. Antony, for instance, attempts to put Caesar's mind at rest, saying of Cassius: 'He is a noble Roman, and well given' (i.ii.194). Caesar, is anything but reassured:

> Would he were fatter! But I fear him not:
> Yet if my name were liable to fear,
> I do not know the man I should avoid
> So soon as that spare Cassius. He reads much,
> He is a great observer, and he looks
> Quite through the deeds of men. He loves no plays,
> As thou dost, Antony; he hears no music.
> Seldom he smiles, and smiles in such a sort
> As if he mock'd himself, and scorn'd his spirit
> That could be mov'd to smile at any thing.
> Such men as he be never at heart's ease
> Whiles they behold a greater than themselves,
> And therefore are they very dangerous.
> I rather tell thee what is to be fear'd
> Than what I fear; for always I am Caesar.
> Come on my right hand, for this ear is deaf,
> And tell me truly what thou think'st of him.
>
> (i.ii.195–211)

The benefit of his perception is lost, however, because he believes himself to be invulnerable – at the very time his human frailty is made abundantly clear. By the end of the next scene Cassius, having concocted the public appeal, is able to feel confident that Brutus will join the conspiracy. Although Cassius has played on Brutus' self-perception as a pillar of Roman democracy, Casca's comment leaves no room for doubt that this is also a true reflection of Brutus' position in Rome:

> O, he sits high in all the people's hearts:
> And that which would appear offence in us,
> His countenance, like richest alchemy,
> Will change to virtue and to worthiness.
>
> (i.iii.157–60)

How does Brutus respond to that most agonising predicament of whether or not to join the conspiracy? During the orchard soliloquy the first words the audience hears are: 'It must be by his death' (ii.i.10). Part of the explanation for the contrasting views of Brutus' analysis of the problem confronting him is that we seem to come in mid-way through the internal debate. It appears that the alternatives have been contemplated and rejected. Is what follows a *post hoc* rationalisation of a decision already arrived at, or does it represent the core of Brutus' reasoning after an interrogation of the issue? Some critics have dismissed Brutus' 'reasoning' as infantile, and even those most sympathetic to him perceive self-deception.

In his analysis of this soliloquy G. Wilson Knight observes that 'it may be noticed that Brutus' speech in point of complexity and condensation of thought and phrase stands out remarkably from a play of a lucidity and crystal transparence of diction unparalleled in Shakespeare'. Knight is unequivocal in condemning Brutus' reasoning, but adds a caveat which makes clear that Brutus has at his disposal a powerful argument which he fails to use:

> Brutus tells himself that Caesar must be assassinated to avoid the dangers contingent on his nature possibly changing after he becomes king. Yet, he says, he has never known him let passion master reason. There is a hopeless confusion: Brutus' strongest method of justifying his act is to assert that the Roman ideal of a commonwealth must not be shattered by the accession of a king, good or bad. Yet, in his confused desire to justify himself, he does not do this, but falls back on a quite indefensible sophistry.[25]

Schanzer examines this argument in great detail, accepts that Brutus is not opposed in principle to a monarch and stresses the cogency of Brutus' argument:

> Shakespeare's Brutus is by no means a doctrinaire republican, in contrast to Plutarch's Brutus, who reproaches Cicero for favouring Octavius, declaring, 'For our predecessors would never abide to be subject to any Master, how gentle or mild soever they were'. Brutus's opposition to kingship rests on his fears of the corrupting effect of the power it bestows, not on the nature of its office. . . . It would seem that, finding nothing in the mere fact of kingship, nor anything in Caesar's past behaviour to justify the assassination, Brutus deludes himself by vastly exaggerating the gap that separates the present from the future Caesar, the dictator from the king. Once this position is taken up, Brutus

has no difficulty in advancing a logical argument for the assassination, and in this he is aided by his metaphor. . . . The argument is quite cogent and contains no confusion, as some commentators have claimed. But it is founded on self-deception.

And Schanzer provides a telling conclusion when he comments:

> By thus putting the justification for the murder on a pragmatic basis Brutus lays the foundation for his later tragedy. Had he been a doctrinaire republican and murdered Caesar to save the republic from kingship he would have been safe, if not from inner conflict, at least from tragic disillusion. For his purpose would have been accomplished. But by justifying the deed to himself and others on the grounds of 'pity to the general wrong of Rome' (3.i.171), the wrong that Caesar may have committed in the future, he puts himself at the mercy of events. For it is only by establishing a government under which the people suffer less wrong than they would have done under Caesar's rule that the murder can, to Brutus, be justified. And what are the consequences as they are depicted in the play?[26]

Another view of the internal debate is provided by Granville-Barker:

> If the argument is supersubtle and unconvincing, why should it not be? It may be that Shakespeare himself is still fumbling to discover how this right-minded man can commit his conscience to murder, and why should his Brutus not be fumbling too? This is how it will seem to an audience, surely.[27]

At the very least this comment serves as a reminder of the contrasting impressions which may be gained from the page and from the stage. Moreover, this observation serves as a valuable counterweight to Norman Rabkin's view that:

> Shakespeare shows us that even the man who attempts to live by reason is governed by irrational elements within himself that he cannot recognize. Thus the great soliloquy in which Brutus contemplates the killing of Caesar begins with a decision already made – 'It must be by his death' – and proceeds through a set of rationalizations that reveal the utter absence of foundation for Brutus' fears.[28]

Turning to the nature of the language employed by Brutus, James R. Siemon makes the observation that: 'In compounding his images out of half-truths and conjectures about Caesar and out of commonplaces about serpents, Brutus stands as an ominous warning of the dramatist's sensitivity to the potential abuses inherent in his chosen verbal medium.'[29] W. O. Scott also emphasises Brutus' dependence on metaphor and analogy to reach his desired conclusion: 'Brutus carries on this persuasion . . . through flagrantly rhetorical means: by application of abstract principles to individual cases, and by argument from analogy.'[30] For Scott, Brutus is a willing victim of his own process of false reasoning.

It is apparent, then, that several critics have censured Brutus for his manifest failure to expose Julius Caesar as a latent tyrant. Indeed, the evidence advanced in the soliloquy points in quite the opposite direction. Yet ironically, if Brutus does force the conclusion he desires, he is, arguably, being too generous in his evaluation of Caesar's past behaviour. This is a line of argument recently advanced by Alexander Leggatt, who reverses the usual critical assessment. For him, Brutus does not distort the facts to reach a pre-determined conclusion, but ignores several acts which condemn Caesar and might serve to validate the assassination:

> What is remarkable is not so much the argument itself (that power corrupts, and therefore even a good man who is about to become powerful should be killed) as Brutus' insistence that there is nothing in Caesar's present behaviour to warrant killing him . . . we have already seen Caesar's arrogance and vanity, and the obsequiousness that surrounds him, in which even Casca joins; we have heard, and so has Brutus, that 'Marullus and Flavius, for pulling scarfs off Caesar's images, are put to silence' (i.ii.282–3). The tyranny Brutus fears as a theoretical possibility in the future is a clear and present danger. Cassius has already insisted on it. Brutus is frequently chided by critics for killing a man for the sake of a theory; but Shakespeare is, I think, less concerned with the quality of Brutus' reasoning than with his inability to start with the evidence under his nose.[31]

The substance of this criticism had been made much earlier by Coleridge, who convicts Shakespeare of failing in historical verisimilitude:

> surely nothing can seem more discordant with our historical preconceptions of Brutus, or more *lowering* to the intellect of this Stoico-Platonic tyrannicide, than the tenets here attributed to *him*, the stern Roman republican; viz., that he would have no objection to a king, or to Caesar, a monarch in Rome, would Caesar be as good a monarch as he now seems disposed to be. How too could Brutus say he finds no personal

cause; i.e. none in Caesar's past conduct as a man? Had he not passed the Rubicon? Entered Rome as a conqueror? Placed his Gauls in the Senate? Shakespeare (it may be said) has not brought these things forward. True! and this is just the ground of my perplexity. What character does Shakespeare mean *his* Brutus to be?[3]2

But whereas Leggatt condemns Shakespeare's Brutus for failing to take proper account of the evidence he encounters in the play, Coleridge blames the dramatist for not making his Brutus more like his historical counterpart and for deliberately excluding or obscuring important historical facts. Someone who rejects these arguments and provides what is perhaps the best defence of Brutus is A. D. Nuttall. He exonerates Brutus from the charges of rationalisation and naïvety, pointing out that 'Brutus goes out of his way to stress the *tenuousness* of his case, pauses on all the weak links in the chain, and this, surely, is almost the opposite of rationalization.' He goes on to argue that 'Brutus' speech is both moving and impressive in its refusal to dress up a political rationale as something more watertight than it really is', concluding with an interpretation of the crucial phrase 'fashion it thus':

> Brutus is not, in fact, proposing to feign a belief and then to execute the fiction in real life. He is saying to himself 'It is no use trying to construct this case with reference to what I know of Caesar, now. Rather, put it this way . . .' To paraphrase thus is indeed to soften the worrying word 'fashion', which obstinately retains a suggestion of fiction. . . . Nevertheless, the main tenor of the idiom is donnishly abstract rather than cynically self-manipulative. It is much closer to the philosopher's 'Let's try the argument this way . . .' than to 'This shall be my motive'. If it is asked, 'Why, then, granting that the Iago-subaudition is only a subaudition, did Shakespeare allow it into the line?' the answer is, perhaps, because he wished to hint that the second state of mind was, in a sinister fashion, latent in the first.[33]

Nevertheless, even this interpretation does not remove the necessity for further analysis of the text and a disentangling of the interweaving elements in a speech which mirrors the play as a whole in its capacity to appear simultaneously simple and complex. Close scrutiny of the soliloquy reveals two facts: Brutus is not motivated by any personal antagonism towards Caesar; any action will be undertaken for the good of Rome. As Brutus expresses the matter:

I know no *personal* cause to spurn at him,
But for the *general*.

(ii.i.11–12)

This fact is followed by a piece of interpretation, namely, the nature of the threat to Rome:

He would be crown'd:
How *that* might *change* his nature, there's the question.

(ii.i.12–13)

The implication is that Caesar does not currently present a threat to Rome – a view evidently not shared by others, including Cassius, Marullus and Flavius. In fact Brutus explicitly acquits Caesar of any suggestion that he has abused this power:

to speak truth of Caesar,
I have not known when his affections sway'd
More than his reason.

(ii.i.19–21)

Caesar's affections or passions, then, have always been kept in check by his reason. This second 'fact' presented to us by Brutus has the status of a fact only within the parameters of Brutus' debate, because the audience, as Leggatt points out, has reason to think differently. What is clear from Brutus' presentation of the facts in the soliloquy is that he has reason to be favourably inclined towards Caesar despite his anxiety about the excessive power and status of the great man. The crucial interpretative feature of the speech is that Caesar *may* be transformed into something intolerable *if* he becomes king. The metaphors and analogies which are interwoven with these two facts, and one interpretive possibility, are more striking for their waywardness than for their relevance. Brutus starts with a fact but does not follow it with direct analysis of the political situation and its likely progression. Rather he evades such careful step by step reasoning by resorting to images and analogies which do not bear the weight required of them. Thus Brutus is both over-generous in giving Caesar his due and under-scrupulous in anticipating his future behaviour. What Shakespeare reveals in this soliloquy is the process of moral contamination which characterises political action. Gratified by the perception of himself as the true guardian of the spirit of Rome, Brutus is cajoled by Cassius into contemplating murder. Brutus attempts to confront a reality which is alien to a refined spirit, flinches, and resorts to dubious reasoning. Inner conflict is manifest in the corrupt use of language. The analogies and images are banal. They are the expression of the subconscious forces at work in Brutus. Hence the critical vituperation to which this soliloquy has given rise. Critics have wanted Brutus' argument to be more compelling, to be more worthy of him. What the dramatist has given his character is everything that Brutus is capable of in the circumstances: he is a man earnestly seeking to be just, but is, in his innermost being, already bent on a course of action which is alien to him. What we see in the isolation of his orchard is not Brutus the constitutional lawyer, but Brutus the man seeking resolution and escape from the 'hideous dream' (ii.i.65). Just as he does later at Philippi, Brutus seeks to free himself from doubt and anguish by launching himself into action. John Wilders reminds us, that the word paradise derives from the Persian word *pairidaeza*, which 'signified a walled garden, park or orchard and there is evidence that Shakespeare thought of such places when he created the temporary retreats from the world into which some of his characters take refuge'.[34] Wilders' interesting discussion does not touch on Brutus' orchard scene but it seems particularly germane to this incident. The moment is rich with suggestion and allusion, there is a feeling of Brutus in Eden, with the serpent playing a particularly insidious role in his 'reason by metaphor' soliloquy. Already having lost sleep (that powerful symbol of mental harmony), he is about to lose his purity of spirit.

Careful analysis suggests, then, a wary and suspicious Brutus, unready to contemplate assassination until 'whet' by Cassius. His anguished state of mind is clearly revealed in his Macbeth-like soliloquy (ii.i.61–9) and in the complaints made by Portia. Brutus is experiencing an emotional push which is stronger than his reason will allow, hence the distortion of language and argument which takes place. It is when reading Cassius' forged appeals that Brutus' feeling of his responsibility to Rome and his place in Roman society becomes manifest – a perception Cassius has so perfectly judged as being the weak point of Brutus' character:

> Shall Rome stand under one man's awe? What, Rome?
> My ancestors did from the streets of Rome
> The Tarquin drive, when he was call'd king.
> 'Speak, strike, redress!' Am I entreated
> To speak, and strike? O Rome, I make thee promise,
> If the redress will follow, thou receivest
> Thy full petition at the hand of Brutus.
>
> (ii.i.52–8)

It is beautifully ironic that Shakespeare's character, unlike his historical counterpart, is not responding to a genuine public appeal at all, but to Cassius' forgeries. However, once Brutus commits himself, his intellectual reservations are forgotten. As he rejects the proposal of oath-taking, he talks as if Caesar were already a full-blown tyrant poised to strike:

> So let high-sighted tyranny range on,
> Till each man drop by lottery.
> (II.i.118–19)

It is as if Brutus engages emotional overdrive to quell his earlier misgivings. He quickly dominates the conspiracy, vetoing the seemingly unanimous proposal that Cicero be invited to join them, and even more significantly the proposal to assassinate Antony. Whereas Cassius advances clear reasons in simple language why Antony cannot be allowed to survive Caesar, Brutus resorts to metaphors that, far from clarifying reality, totally obscure it. The ideas of Antony as 'but a limb of Caesar' (II.i.165) and of the assassination as a sacrifice in which Caesar is carved 'as a dish fit for the gods' (II.i.173) are hideous distortions. The integrity which Brutus values so highly has already been stained by his premature commitment to the conspiracy. In order to disguise this awareness even from himself he dismisses all opposition and resistance to his will.

At the turning-point in the play, when Antony's servant enters after the assassination, there is a marked contrast between the confidence of Brutus and the unease of Cassius:

> *Bru.* I know that we shall have him well to friend.
> *Cas.* I wish we may: but yet have I a mind
> That fears him much; and my misgiving still
> Falls shrewdly to the purpose.
> (III.i.143–6)

After Antony has made his long emotional speech over the body of Caesar, Brutus attempts to mollify him, promising:

> Our reasons are so full of good regard,
> That were you, Antony, the son of Caesar,
> You should be satisfied.
> (III.i.224–6)

In contrast, Cassius first employs the bait of political advancement:

Your voice shall be as strong as any man's
In the disposing of new dignities.

　　　　　　　　　　　　　　(III.i.177–8)

And follows it up by demanding to know his intentions:

I blame you not for praising Caesar so;
But what compact mean you to have with us?
Will you be prick'd in number of our friends,
Or shall we on, and not depend on you?

　　　　　　　　　　　　　　(III.i.214–17)

These contrasting evaluations of Antony reach a critical point when he requests the right to speak at Caesar's funeral. Brutus' response is immediate and unequivocal – 'You shall, Mark Antony' (III.i.231) – whereas Cassius is staggered by this willingness even to entertain such a proposal:

[*Aside.*] You know not what you do. Do not consent
That Antony speak in his funeral.
Know you how much the people may be mov'd
By that which he will utter?

　　　　　　　　　　　　　　(III.i.232–5)

Brutus' argument has a certain logic – that Antony's role will be strictly circumscribed and that public relations will be improved by Caesar's being granted 'all true rites and lawful ceremonies' (III.i.241) – but it involves a dreadful risk which the politically more astute Cassius does not want to take. What characterises the exchange, as it does later at Sardis, is Brutus' refusal to give any credence to Cassius' view, and the latter's willingness to be overruled against his better judgement. He never agrees with Brutus, he rather endures his dominance. It is a strange irony that Cassius is so calculating and devious in drawing Brutus into the conspiracy, but thereafter allows him absolute sway. Brutus always has an argument but its appeal is invariably an abstract one, not founded on practical considerations. The dispute over whether to fight at Sardis or Philippi is instructive. Brutus' dubious argument is clinched with a metaphor:

Bru.　Our legions are brim-full, our cause is ripe.
　　　　The enemy increaseth every day;
　　　　We, at the height, are ready to decline.
　　　　There is a tide in the affairs of men,

> Which, taken at the flood, leads on to fortune;
> Omitted, all the voyage of their life
> Is bound in shallows and in miseries.
> On such a full sea are we now afloat,
> And we must take the current when it serves,
> Or lose our ventures.
>
> *Cas.*   Then, with your will, go on;
>   (IV.iii.214–23)

Despite the greater enthusiasm that has been expressed for Antony's Forum speech, Brutus has had many distinguished defenders. Ernest Schanzer for instance comments: 'The whole speech is as shrewdly contrived and, as the response of the people shows, quite as effective as Antony's.'[35] And John Palmer claims that: 'He makes no appeal to the emotions of his audience. His speech consists of a series of terse, antithetical sentences, conveying precisely the idea he has in mind. It is Euclidean in its logic, Tacitean in its tidiness and brevity.'[36] A contrary augument has been advanced by Granville-Barker, who claims that Brutus' success arises from what he *is* rather than from what he *says*.[37] Whereas Antony's speech is a masterpiece of conscious manipulation, Brutus' finely phrased oration is genuinely presented as a straightforward justification for the assassination. It does possess a fatal flaw, but one that Brutus does not consciously conceal from the crowd: he conceals it from himself. He presents no evidence of Caesar's ambition; it is pure assertion. Set against his hatred of Caesar's ambition is his love of the man. Antony is able to reverse the emotional current by casting doubt on the ambition (emphasising Caesar's role as public servant and tender-hearted leader) and playing up the element of personal affection and, concomitantly, personal betrayal – feelings much more accessible to the commonalty. His unfair 'honourable men' is, of course, a masterpiece of rhetorical construction and psychological audacity, as it enables him to impeach the honour of 'the noblest Roman of them all' (v.v.68)

How any man could place faith in his own judgement after the devastating reversal suffered by Brutus in the Forum scene is astonishing. But, when we next encounter him at Sardis he is all set to chastise Cassius and make the final decision that will lead to the downfall of the conspiracy. From the earliest days of recorded critical comment the quarrel scene has been extolled as one of the highpoints of the play. For Schanzer it 'is in many ways the most important scene in the play. Not only is it here that Brutus's tragic disillusion is most fully revealed to us, but the scene also crystallises the play's main moral issue, the rival claims of personal relations and the *res publica*.[38] John Palmer shrewdly draws attention to the significance of the scene for effecting an important shift in the emotional pressure felt by the audience: 'it secures for Brutus and Cassius, despite the pitiful ruin of their enterprise and yet more pitiful collapse of their integrity of mind and purpose, a sympathy which illumines all the concluding scenes of the tragedy'.[39] Yet despite widespread recognition of the great power, excitement and human truth of this scene, it is, too, the moment in the play which has resulted in the most damning condemnation of the character of Brutus, who has been seen as egotistical, overbearing and hypocritical – a viewpoint recently expressed by James R. Siemon for example.[40] Some comments have already been made on the announcement of Portia's death and Brutus' response to it. Suffice it to add here that when the audience hears Brutus tell Cassius of Portia's death any antagonism that has built up by reason of his superior tone and impatient manner is promptly dissipated. Here is a man sick at heart and the audience recognises it. This emotional shift is completed by the parting of the two men at the end of the scene. Characterised by an extreme simplicity of diction, with the simple 'good night' repeated six times, and Cassius referring to Brutus as 'my lord' and the latter responding with 'good brother', the exchange conveys great emotional intensity. The reiteration of the word 'good' and the sense of longing for emotional harmony achieved through so few and such simple words, including Brutus' reiteration 'Noble, noble, Cassius', is astounding:

Cas.	No more. Good night.
	Early to-morrow will we rise, and hence.
Bru.	Lucius!

[Enter Lucius.]

	My gown. [*Exit Lucius.*]
	Farewell, good Messala.
	Good night, Titinius. Noble, noble Cassius,
	Good night, and good repose.
Cas.	O my dear brother,
	This was an ill beginning of the night.
	Never come such division 'tween our souls!
	Let it not, Brutus.

[Enter Lucius, with the gown.]

Bru.	Everything is well.
Cas.	Good night, my lord.
Bru.	Good night, good brother.
Tit., Mes.	Good night, Lord Brutus.
Bru.	Farewell, everyone.

(IV.iii.228–37)

The softening of audience response to Brutus is complete when Brutus engages in an exchange with Lucius. Leggatt, who, in general, is highly critical of Brutus, makes the following observation:

> When Brutus is dealing with equals, he is controlled, on display, and somewhat overbearing. Alone with his servant, he becomes unexpectedly gentle. Two details matter: Brutus is in his gown, and Lucius, unlike the servants of Caesar, has a name. For the first and only time in the play Brutus admits to having made a mistake:

> > Look, Lucius, here's the book I sought for so;
> > I put it in the pocket of my gown.
> > *Luc.* I was sure your lordship did not give it me.
> > *Bru.* Bear with me, good boy, I am much forgetful.
> > (iv.iii.251–4)

In its smaller way, 'I am much forgetful' is moving as Lear's 'I am old and foolish' is. Brutus, who has taken on the destiny of Rome with a masterful sense of purpose and supreme wrong-headedness, is now hesitant and apologetic with a servant. What from another man would be commands are shy requests.

In the last act the two sides of Brutus' character once again make themselves felt. The assertive, almost self-righteous, Brutus is revealed in his exchange with Octavius:

> *Oct.* I was not born to die on Brutus' sword.
> *Bru.* O, if thou wert the noblest of thy strain,
> Young man, thou could'st not die more honourable.
> (v.i.58–60)

And the mixture of self-contradiction and assurance is present in his denunciation of suicide as 'cowardly' followed by this confident assertion:

> No, Cassius, no: think not, thou noble Roman,
> That ever Brutus will go bound to Rome;
> He bears too great a mind.
> (v.i.111–13)

But no sooner are these lines uttered than we experience another emotional shift with what must be the loveliest parting in the whole of Shakespeare (v.i.117–22). A further oscillation in the emotional pendulum occurs when Titinius announces that the advantage gained over Octavius has been lost because 'Brutus gave the word too early' (v.iii.5) – something which is never recognised by Brutus. Rather, on encountering the dead body of Cassius, he attributes their overthrow to Caesar's spirit:

> O Julius Caesar, thou art mighty yet!
> Thy spirit walks abroad, and turns our swords
> In our own proper entrails.
>   (v.iii.94–6)

Some critics discern an ambiguity in Brutus' response to Cassius' death. Leggatt, for instance, comments: 'Brutus' reaction to Cassius' death, or rather his refusal to react, makes us wonder if he is retreating from feeling or covering up the lack of it.'[41] And this curious sense of ambivalence continues with Brutus' last few comments. First there is the wonderfully domestic touch in Brutus' appeal to Volumnius –

>   Good Volumnius,
> Thou know'st that we two went to school together:
> Even for that our love of old, I prithee
> Hold thou my sword-hilts, whilst I run on it.

Then there is his delight in the loyalty of his friends – but the audience is faintly conscious of an irony here as Brutus fails to recognise his own disloyalty to Caesar:

> Farewell to thee too, Strato. – Countrymen,
> My heart doth joy that yet in all my life
> I found no man but he was true to me.

Likewise Brutus' confident assertion that history will vindicate him hardly proved to be justified:

> I shall have glory by this losing day
> More than Octavius and Mark Antony
> By this vile conquest shall attain unto.
>   (v.v.25–38)

If these lines, uttered by Brutus, were the last reference to him in the play it would be difficult to see him in other than an ironic light. But Mark

Antony's generous encomium concludes with his assessment of the nature of Brutus the man:

> This was the noblest Roman of them all.
> All the conspirators save only he
> Did that they did in envy of great Caesar;
> He only, in a general honest thought
> And common good to all, made one of them.
> His life was gentle, and the elements
> So mix'd in him, that Nature might stand up
> And say to all the world, 'This was a man!'
>   (v.v.68–75)

There is a feeling that Brutus suppresses his natural propensities in aspiring to epitomise the Roman ideal of public service. Spontaneity is sacrificed to honour. Just like Caesar, he fails to recognise the incongruities and misjudgements which inevitably arise from the emasculation of the private man. Perhaps this is the key to the dilemma Shakespeare encountered in the historical Brutus – a dilemma which most critics feel remains in the play. The rigidity of the code to which Brutus is responding blunts his capacity to see his way through problems. He appears positively obtuse on several occasions, totally failing to see the inconsistency in his arguments and behaviour. The self-discipline needed for the attainment of his position as the man above reproach obstructs his natural acuity. No final verdict on Brutus is possible: reactions to Shakespeare's character will vary from one production to another or among individuals coming to the same text. Shakespeare's character is a political failure, at the very least, accelerating, and at the very worst creating, the conditions he seeks to avert. And in the end he seems unaware of what he has done and how he went wrong. But for all his errors of judgement, his fallacious arguments which have been guided more by metaphor than logic, there remains a feeling of pity for the man who was possessed of tenderness and humanity, who believed that what he did was a service required by Rome.

If sympathy for Brutus continues to oscillate up to the moment of his death, the situation with regard to Cassius is very different. Despite a capacity for manipulation and a readiness to plot the murder of Caesar on the grounds of personal antagonism, Cassius becomes an increasingly sympathetic figure during the fifth act. Admiration for his political acumen begins at ii.i.155 and gathers force as he continually makes decisions which are countermanded by Brutus. The need to kill Antony along with Caesar, or, at least, to prevent him from speaking at Caesar's funeral, and to fight at

Sardis rather than Philippi, are all sound judgements. Personal sympathy, however, really gathers force during the quarrel scene, where his emotional dependence on Brutus and his longing for a truly reciprocated friendship become apparent. There is immense appeal in this weakness, partly because Cassius is such a vigorous and manly character. His diction is clear and strong, his passion, even when it spills over into jealousy, is ardent. Anyone who has seen the right kind of actor play Cassius will realise the immensity of his appeal. Such was Emrys James' success in this role in the RSC's 1983–4 production. He was the most compelling character in the play. Even so, Cassius, like Julius Caesar and Brutus, has his admirers and detractors. Granville-Barker, for instance, takes a harsh view of him:

> His death is of a piece with his whole reckless life. He kills himself because he will not wait another minute to verify the tale his bondman tells him of Titinius' capture. He ends passionately and desperately – but still grasping his standard. Even at this moment he is as harsh to Pindarus as Brutus is gentle to his boy Lucius and the bondman who serves him:
>
> > Come hither, sirrah:
> > In Parthia did I take thee prisoner;
> > And then I swore thee, saving of thy life,
> > That whatsoever I did bid thee do,
> > Thou shouldst attempt it.
>
> His last words are as bare and ruthless.
>
> > Caesar, thou art reveng'd
> > Even with the sword that kill'd thee.
>
> Pindarus' four lines that follow may seem frigid and formal.[42]

In contrast G. Wilson Knight detects an attractive character. Beginning with Caesar's analysis of Cassius (I.ii.191–207), he comments:

> The description is not one to be ashamed of. Cassius has profound understanding, a rich personality. He is very sincere. He claims, rightly, to have nothing in him of the flatterer or scandalmonger: he is no 'common laugher' like Lucio (I.ii.72–8). His seriousness makes him sombre, gloomy, ashamed of all trivialities. Smiles, plays, music – all are barred. Instead, we have knowledge of men, books, restlessness of

temperament. . . . Brutus is still hampering success by continued regard for his 'honour'. Cassius, less scrupulous, shows, as always, more warmness of heart. Cassius is always in touch with realities – of love, of conspiracy, of war: Brutus is ever most at home with his ethical abstractions. He treasures to his heart the 'justice' of his cause.[43]

Alexander Leggatt, also, expresses admiration for Cassius and makes a revealing comment when describing his relationship with Titinius:

He and Titinius literally die for each other. We have seen Cassius pleading for Brutus' love and never quite getting it. All we see of his relationship with Titinius, earlier in v.iii., is two men simply working together, making no parade of their friendship. The revelation of the depth of that friendship is a flash of the unexpected, a touch of unprogrammed humanity in a world of controlled display.[44]

Despite the contrasting nature of some of these evaluations, it is hard to think of another character in the plays of Shakespeare who has so much individuality as Cassius. Everything about him seems natural and authentic, including his wild emotional swings and passionate outbursts. There is something not quite dignified about Cassius; the schoolboy frequently shows through the man. For instance, in the pre-battle quarrel with Octavius and Antony, Cassius denounces the latter just like a schoolboy.

> Antony,
> The posture of your blows are yet unknown;
> But for your words, they rob the Hybla bees,
> And leave them honeyless.
>
> (v.i.32–5)

And a little later in the dialogue Antony's riposte to Cassius' jibes seems perfectly apt:

> *Cas.* A peevish school-boy, worthless of such honour,
> Join'd with a masker and a reveller.
> *Ant.* Old Cassius still!
>
> (v.i.61–3)

As they break off the parley in readiness to fight we have a glimpse of the tempestuous nature that earlier dared the lightning to strike him:

Why now, blow wind, swell billow, and swim bark!
The storm is up, and all is on the hazard.

(v.i.67–8)

Moments later, with the most appealing simplicity, Cassius reveals that it is his birthday. Expressing a compulsion to see a pattern in his life, he reluctantly (as an Epicurean) acknowledges a force like destiny or fate at work. Even so, he wishes to put the historical record straight:

Cas. This is my birth-day; on this very day
        Was Cassius born. Give me thy hand, Messala:
        Be thou my witness that against my will
        (As Pompey was) am I compell'd to set
        Upon one battle all our liberties.
        You know that I held Epicurus strong,
        And his opinion; now I change my mind,
        And partly credit things that do presage.
        Coming from Sardis, on our former ensign
        Two mighty eagles fell, and there they perch'd,
        Gorging and feeding from our soldiers' hands,
        Who to Philippi here consorted us.
        This morning are they fled away and gone,
        And in their steads do ravens, crows, and kites
        Fly o'er our heads, and downward look on us,
        As we were sickly prey; their shadows seem
        A canopy most fatal, under which
        Our army lies, ready to give up the ghost.
Mes. Believe not so.
Cas.   I but believe it partly,
        For I am fresh of spirit, and resolv'd
        To meet all perils very constantly.

(v.i.72–92)

Perhaps in his final farewell to Brutus, Cassius achieves a dignity, although it is not a word which is most naturally associated with him:

For ever, and for ever, farewell, Brutus.
If we do meet again, we'll smile indeed;
If not, 'tis true, this parting was well made.

(v.i.120–2)

What is felt here is the tremor of human warmth, something manly and wholly genuine. Then that reckless quality reveals itself again, the rush of blood that took Cassius to the brink of panic moments before the assassination. Unwilling to wait for confirmation of Titinius' fate, Cassius seeks his own death. Had the historical Cassius been less precipitate their cause might still have prevailed, as it was the loss of his disciplined hold over his men that led to the final defeat. Even Cassius' epitaph does not sound quite right. Described, along with Titinius, by Brutus as 'The last of all the Romans' (v.iii.99), he seems the least Roman of the Romans in this play, appearing, above all, a man.

As in the case of Casca, however, critical commentary has raised questions about the consistency of Cassius' character. The paradox of a devious Cassius who entices Brutus into the conspiracy only to become dominated by him for the rest of the play is perplexing, forming part of a wider problem of the emergence of the noble Cassius towards the end of the play.[45] Richard Levin sees the evolution of Cassius as a case of artistic failure. Drawing on Ralph Rader's conception of 'the unintended and unavoidable negative consequence of the artist's positive constructive intention',[46] Levin makes his case as follows:

> the change in Cassius can be explained as the 'unintended consequence' of Shakespeare's primary 'constructive intention' to make Brutus a sympathetic and admirable tragic hero. In the opening scenes Cassius is portrayed as a Machiavellian manipulator of Brutus in order to establish a contrast with Brutus's much more honourable motives for joining the conspiracy and to emphasize his essential innocence. But in the last two acts, when their fates are inextricably linked, Cassius must become a nobler man, especially in the depth and sincerity of his love for Brutus, in order to validate Brutus's own feelings for their friendship and thus to enhance our tragic empathy with him, as can be seen very clearly in their poignant parting before the battle (5.1) and in his reaction to Cassius's death (5.3).[47]

Mark Antony

Plutarch records that Antony was physically impressive: 'he had a goodly thicke beard, a broad forehead, crooke nosed and there appeared such a manly looke in his countenaunce, as is commonly seene in Hercules pictures, stamped or graven in mettell'. Antony, whose family traced its ancestry back to Hercules, attempted to accentuate this resemblance – even wearing his garments in a way reminiscent of the ancient hero. According to the historian, his virtues were courage, conviviality and liberality. Immensely popular with the soldiers, he had the rare ability to mingle and drink with them as their equal while retaining their respect. As Plutarch expresses it:

> things that seeme intollerable in other men, as to boast commonly, to jeast with one or other, to drinke like a good fellow with every body, to sit with the soldiers when they dine, and to eate and drinke with them souldier-like: it is incredible what wonderfull love it wanne him amongest them. . . . But besides all this, that which most procured his rising and advauncement, was his liberalitie, who gave all to the souldiers, and kept nothing for him selfe.

These attractive traits, however, were more than counterbalanced by his vices: he was corrupt, lecherous and cruel.

This duality in Antony's nature is clearly demonstrated by two incidents. The first, which won him great praise, was the bestowing of a magnificent coat to cover Brutus' body on the funeral pyre. The soldier entrusted with the task attempted to steal the coat and was promptly executed. The contrast between Antony's magnanimity and viciousness is revealed, also, by comparing his treatment of Enobarbus and Cicero. When deserted by the former, Antony expressed his sorrow and sent Enobarbus' treasure after him. Cicero, however, aroused Antony's bitter antagonism by denouncing him in his Philippics. When Antony formed the triumvirate with Lepidus and Octavius they spent three days haggling over the proscription list. Antony fought hard to have Cicero executed, and he did not stop there: he had the body dismembered and the head and hands put on display. Moreover, 'when the murtherers brought him Ciceroes head and hand cut of, he beheld them a long time with great joy, and laughed heartily, and that oftentimes for the great joy he felt'. Plutarch comments on this event more than once with burning indignation:

> Antonius suffered his Uncle by his mother's side to be slaine, that he might have his will of Cicero to kill him: a thing so damnable, wicked, and cruell of it selfe, that he hardlie deserved to have bene pardoned, though he had killed Cicero, to have saved his Uncles life.

At another point Plutarch describes Cicero's capture and murder:

> So Cicero being three score and foure yeares of age, thrust his necke out of the litter, and had his head cut of by Antonius commaundement, and his hands also, which wrote the Orations (called the Philippians) against

him: ... When these poore dismembred members were brought to Rome, Antonius ... commaunded his head and his hands should straight be set up over the pulpit for Orations, in the place called Rostra. This was a fearefull and horrible sight unto the Romanes, who thought they saw not Ciceroes face, but an image of Antonius life and disposicion:

The dramatist provides a chilling proscription scene but there is no reference to the mutilation of Cicero, and Antony's joyful response to the news. Commenting on Antony's greatest military triumph, Plutarch exposes his political motivation:

For the greatest and most famous exployte Antonius ever did in warres (to wit, the warre in the which he overthrew Cassius and Brutus) was begon to no other ende, but to deprive his contriemen of their libertie and freedom.[48]

The Antony who emerges from the pages of Plutarch, therefore, is a dissolute and vicious individual whose attractive features are so few in comparison with his vices that rather than redeeming him they merely serve to mitigate the feeling that he was a thoroughly bad man.

There is nothing to suggest the construction of Antony's Forum speech in Plutarch. An uncertain, though probable, source for the dramatist was Appian's *The Civil Wars*. The section dealing with Antony's speech at Caesar's funeral might have offered numerous suggestions for Shakespeare. First, Appian records how Antony opened his oration by referring to his role as 'Consul, of a Consul, friend, of a friend, and kinsman, of a kinsman (for Antony was partly his kinsman)'. Shakespeare's Antony insists: 'He was my friend, faithful and just to me' (iii.ii.87). And this element of friendship is the fulcrum on which the oration is balanced, as Antony insinuates a contrast between Caesar's loyalty as a friend and Brutus' disloyalty and betrayal of friendship. Secondly, Appian draws attention to the way in which Antony used Caesar's body as a focal point: 'Antonie directed his countenance and hands to Caesars body' and mixed 'pitie and indignation' – key features adopted by Shakespeare. Thirdly, Antony invited the citizens to 'purge' themselves of 'this unkindnesse'. Shakespeare says of the wound inflicted by Brutus: 'This was the most unkindest cut of all' (iii.ii.185). Fourthly, after Antony had stirred the crowd to a passion, creating 'an uproare' and swearing that he was 'ready to revenge', he 'waxed colde, and recanted hys wordes'. Shakespeare's Antony, having created the same hysteria, exerts exactly the same restraint:

Good friends, sweet friends, let me not stir you up
To such a sudden flood of mutiny.

                              (III.ii.212–13)

Fifthly, Antony, having 'gyrded' his gown 'that he might better stirre his handes', sang a hymn to Caesar, then 'rehearsed the warres, the fights, the victories, the nations that he had subdued to his Countrey, and the great booties that he had sent, making every one to be a marvell'. Shakespeare's Antony does not provide this catalogue of victories, but at one point makes the critical observation:

He hath brought many captives home to Rome,
Whose ransoms did the general coffers fill:
Did this in Caesar seem ambitious?

                              (III.ii.90–2)

He reminds his audience of Caesar's triumphs but turns them into acts of altruism rather than a quest for personal glory. Later in the speech he refers to one of Caesar's greatest victories but does so in a way that makes it appear an inadvertent reference, made only because it is associated with the gown worn by Caesar when he was struck down:

If you have tears, prepare to shed them now.
You all do know this mantle. I remember
The first time ever Caesar put it on;
'Twas on a summer's evening in his tent,
That day he overcame the Nervii.

                              (III.ii.171–5)

The intense realisation of this event – ''Twas on a summer's evening in his tent' – and the subtlety of the reference to one specific triumph exert a much more powerful hold on the imagination than the enumeration of victories, but it is hard to believe that Shakespeare was not influenced in this respect by Appian's description. Next Appian recounts how Antony:

falling into moste vehement affections, uncovered Caesars body, hold-ing up his vesture with a speare, cut with the woundes, and redde with the bloude of the chiefe Ruler, by the which the people lyke a Quire, did sing lamentation unto him, and by this passion were againe repleate with ire.

Shakespeare's Antony, of course, makes much greater use of the gown, specifying the perpetrators of each rent in the bloodstained garment. But even this detail may have been suggested by Appian, who says of Antony:

> Then made he Caesar hymselfe to speake as it were in a lamentable sort, to howe many of his enemies he hadde done good by name, and of the killers themselves to say as in an admiration, *did I save them that have killed me?* This the people could not abide, calling to remembraunce, that all the kyllers (only Decimus except) were of Pompeys faction, and subdued by hym, to whom, in stead of punishment, he had given promotion of offices, governments of provinces and armies, and thought Decimus worthy to be made his heyre and son by adoption, and yet conspired hys death.

Clearly the significance of this description is to emphasise the ingratitude and disloyalty of the men to whom Caesar had been benefactor. Shakespeare imaginatively enters into the mind of the historical Antony, perceives his intent, and devises a more effective means for achieving the desired emotional pressure. Shakespeare's Antony follows Appian's Antony in the next move and goes beyond him. Appian tells how Antony brought:

> the Image of Caesar, made of waxe, for hys body it selfe lying flat in the Litter, could not be seene. Hys picture was by a devise turned about, and .xxiii. wounds wer shewed over al his body, and his face horrible to behold. The people seeing this pittifull picture, coulde beare the dolour no longer, but thronged togyther, and beset the Senate house, wherein Caesar was kylled, and set it a fyre, and the kyllers that fledde for their lives.

Shakespeare's Antony reveals the body itself:

> Kind souls, what weep you when you but behold
> Our Caesar's vesture wounded? Look you here!
> Here is himself, marr'd, as you see, with traitors.
> (III.ii.197–9)

The response in both cases is explosive – but whereas in Appian's account the crowd storm off to take their destructive revenge, including the horrible killing of Cinna, whom they 'cruelly tore him to peeces, and lefte not one parte to be put in grave',[49] Shakespeare's crowd is restrained in order to hear the will – the will which establishes them as Caesar's heirs. A will which, in all the historical accounts, had been made known before the funeral. A comparison of Appian's account with Shakespeare's powerful scene reveals the way in which Shakespeare submerged himself imaginatively into the historical situation while simultaneously translating these events into a dramatic structure with all its possibilities and limitations. What emerges from an examination of the source material, and the way in which it was used by Shakespeare, is the sense of a scrupulous mind ranging over the details and having its imagination kindled by excitement. The contrast between what enters the crucible of the imagination and what emerges from it generally leaves the reader awed, but it is perhaps possible to catch a glimpse of the process of metamorphosis.

Perhaps the most striking contrast between Plutarch's Antony and Shakespeare's is that the dramatist skilfully preserves a balance that can allow Antony to emerge as the hero of the piece – as a glance at the history of the play in performance demonstrates. The historian gives Antony his due but ultimately damns him. Perhaps the essence of Shakespeare's Antony is that he is, in the words of David Daiches, 'the man without innocence, the man who knows how to unite his personal affections with his political ambitions'.[50] Antony exhibits no political *values* at all; his attachment to Caesar seems purely personal; having achieved his goal of thwarting the republican conspiracy he quickly sets about gaining power for himself and ensuring the destruction of his political opponents. Antony can even put his emotional suffering to practical use, as he does in the Forum scene. He is, as Granville-Barker puts it, 'a born opportunist, and we see him best in the light of his great opportunity. . . . Up to the time when he faces the triumphant conspirators he speaks just thirty-three words.'[51] It is ironic that though this supreme opportunist steals the initiative from Brutus and Cassius through his magnificent oratory, and turns the tide at Philippi to guarantee on the battlefield what has been achieved in the Forum, by the end of the play he is visibly being elbowed aside by a relatively insignificant young man, Octavius Caesar.

Octavius
The Life of Octavius Caesar was added to the 1603 edition of Plutarch's *Lives*, and was almost certainly read by Shakespeare, but it may not have been available to him during the writing of *Julius Caesar*. Yet the character of whom we see so little in the play is, in embryo, the character Shakespeare portrays in fine detail in *Antony and Cleopatra*. If Antony explodes on to the scene, Octavius simply insinuates himself into it: 'he appears three times' and 'speaks some thirty lines'.[52] It is astonishing that within such a small compass Shakespeare conveys an entire character: cold, self-contained,

assertive and absolutely determined. During the proscription scene he neutralises the Antony who moments earlier appeared to be totally in control. Previously dominant, Antony is now surprisingly held in check: he sounds rough and awkward when set against the new voice, uncharismatic but precise and strangely threatening. A line and a half in the opening three lines of the proscription scene are enough to make this distinctive new presence clearly felt.

> *Ant.*   These many then shall die; their names are prick'd.
> *Oct.*   Your brother too must die; consent you, Lepidus?
> *Lep.*   I do consent –
> *Oct.*   Prick him down, Antony.
>
> (iv.i.1–3)

When Lepidus, humbly accepting the role of messenger, asks where he should return with Caesar's will, it is Octavius who authoritatively responds: 'Or here or at the Capitol' (iv.i.11). As Antony proceeds to make long speeches disparaging Lepidus and displaying a loutish arrogance, Octavius confines himself to brief replies always to the point and delivered with an air of aloof superiority. Antony's attempt at assertiveness seems strangely ineffectual – 'Octavius, I have seen more days than you;' (iv.i.18) – and Octavius has the last word.

The note of competitiveness and the contrast between bluster and urbanity is again present when Octavius reappears at the opening of Act v. Octavius is keen to show that Antony is wrong in his judgement about the strategy of their adversaries, but as he glows with undisguised pleasure the audience is aware that Antony's military assessment coincides with that of Cassius. Antony feels obliged to defend his judgement, but in doing so he misrepresents the motives of his enemies and fails to sound convincing. Then comes the issue of who is to lead the more prestigious right flank, which Antony, quite naturally, claims for himself. The rebuff is startling:

> *Ant.*   Octavius, lead your battle softly on
>   Upon the left hand of the even field.
> *Oct.*   Upon the right hand I. Keep thou the left.
> *Ant.*   Why do you cross me in this exigent?
> *Oct.*   I do not cross you; but I will do so.
>
> (v.i.16–20)

Interestingly, in this scene, Octavius assumes the title 'Caesar' and Brutus confirms it.

The immaturity of Octavius becomes apparent only in the confrontation with Brutus and Cassius. Perhaps this is because there is no meeting of minds between these adversaries:

> *Bru.* Words before blows: is it so, countrymen?
> *Oct.* Not that we love words better, as you do.
> (v.i.27–8)

The exchanges between Antony, Cassius and Brutus have a personal, intimate feel, whereas Octavius' contribution sounds impertinent:

> *Oct.* Come, come, the cause. If arguing make us sweat,
> The proof of it will turn to redder drops.
> Look,
> I draw a sword against conspirators.
> When think you that the sword goes up again?
> Never, till Caesar's three and thirty wounds
> Be well aveng'd; or till another Caesar
> Have added slaughter to the sword of traitors.
> *Bru.* Caesar, thou canst not die by traitors' hands,
> Unless thou bring'st them with thee.
> *Oct.*   So I hope.
> I was not born to die on Brutus' sword.
> (v.i.48–58)

Although Octavius loses his part of the ensuing battle he emerges with his self-esteem and composure intact, calculatingly commandeering Brutus' men: 'All that serv'd Brutus, I will entertain them' (v.v.60). Having creamed off the military leadership, Octavius then takes charge of Brutus' funeral arrangements and closes the play like the master of ceremonies he is:

> According to his virtue let us use him,
> With all respect and rites of burial.
> Within my tent his bones to-night shall lie,
> Most like a soldier, order'd honourably.
> So call the field to rest, and let's away,
> To part the glories of this happy day.
> (v.v.76–81)

Actors on the stage of history

Caesar, Brutus, Cassius and Antony are all drawn on a grand scale: Shakespeare conveys a vivid sense of personalities with distinctive idiosyncrasies and weaknesses. Perceptions of these characters emanate not only from their own words and actions, but from the comments and assessments of others. For instance, despite several attempts by individuals to show Caesar in a bad light, the images invoked reveal how enormous is his stature in Rome. Only Casca manages to deflate the image. Paradoxically the hollowness of Caesar's 'greatness' is exposed by his own desperate attempt to live up to the image. The feeling conveyed is that the Julius Caesar observed in the play is a lesser man now than he was earlier in his career: the man has been absorbed by the image; now subject to flattery and superstition, Caesar shows only flashes of his former insight and courage. When Antony expresses shock at the sight of the corpse:

O mighty Caesar! dost thou lie so low?
Are all thy conquests, glories, triumphs, spoils,
Shrunk to this little measure?
(III.i.148–50)

his words could apply metaphorically to the living Caesar seen on the stage. Likewise Antony's encomium on Brutus portrays a character who transcends the Brutus seen on the stage. Shakespeare's audience has seen only the anguished Brutus who, drawn into the conspiracy, struggles to justify the assassination to himself by creating a mental formulation which will assuage his conscience. His admirable qualities as public man of unquestioned integrity stem from the same source as his vulnerability: his sense of the Roman world and his place in it as servant and protector of its ideals. As Ann Molan puts it: 'For Brutus, "Rome" as an ideal can almost be defined as that for which the personal must be sacrificed.'[53] In his assessment of Brutus' character, and his failure, William Hazlitt argued:

Those who mean well themselves think well of others, and fall a prey to their security. That humanity and honesty which dispose men to resist injustice and tyranny render them unfit to cope with the cunning and power of those who are opposed to them.[54]

Dowden, on the other hand, gave a different slant to the commitment of Brutus:

It is idealists who create a political terror; they are free from all desire for blood-shedding; but to them the lives of men and women are accidents; the lives of ideas are the true realities; and, armed with an abstract principle and a suspicion, they perform deeds which are at once beautiful and hideous.[55]

This commitment enables Brutus to kill his friend – but he has to represent it as sacrifice rather than murder. It also deprives him of the ruthlessness to undertake the politically expedient killing of Antony. Indeed his scrupulosity presents Antony, albeit inadvertently, with a platform to defeat the conspirators. Ironically, awareness of his own integrity and doubt about the moral rectitude of Cassius lead him to assume control of the conspiracy and to override the opinions of his brother-in-arms who is politically and militarily more experienced and astute. Purity of intention is all that matters to Brutus, and his evident dismay in his encounters with the ghost of Caesar reveals that he has never been able completely to satisfy himself that the murder was justified. Added to this anguish is awareness of his sacrifice of Portia, whom he loves dearly, to his public responsibilities. Most critics maintain that one of the two announcements of Portia's death is redundant. But the dual presentation enables the audience to experience the suffering and inner turmoil in his quarrel with Cassius, and later to allow him to present a stoic, public response when he receives the news for the second time. In a recent Stratford production (1987), Roger Allam effectively conveyed a sense of Brutus' anguish at the beginning of the scene by burning a letter and crumbling the ashes in his hand. Brutus, then, emerges as the 'noblest Roman', as a man suited to serve as a living model of Roman *gravitas*, an essential contributor to the political life of the state, but wholly unsuited to the role of conspirator and political leader. As Ann Molan expresses it: 'The play makes it clear that his primacy in the conspiracy is accorded not because his principles demand respect but because the singular charisma or grace of *his* life draws men's hearts. . . . Brutus is the singular man in Rome thought capable of obliterating the singular Caesar.'[56]

Perhaps the most remarkable feature of Shakespeare's presentation of Cassius is the way in which he moves from being an unattractive political manipulator at the beginning of the play to the highly sympathetic character at the end. But whereas our response to Cassius changes by experiencing different aspects of his character, Shakespeare's Antony is a veritable chameleon. He displays a warm emotional commitment to Caesar and determination to avenge his murdered friend. What Antony does not convey, however, is any feeling of a commitment to Roman values. He is a political opportunist who exhibits astonishing calculation from the moment of Caesar's death. His Forum speech reveals great insight into the minds of the common people and a masterly ability to manipulate language and feelings. It is the contrast between this public performance (and Shakespeare enables the audience to detect and savour every moment of the control of the crowd) and his display of cold, almost uncouth, cynicism which makes the proscription scene so shocking. If Antony appears as the supreme politician, unfettered by values and ideals, he seems warm-hearted when contrasted with Octavius Caesar. Although Shakespeare presents no more than a cameo of Octavius, his characterisation reveals stubbornness and a steely ambition allied with suavity and a strong sense of superiority. The time gap between the writing of *Julius Caesar* and *Antony and Cleopatra* is astonishingly wide given the way in which Shakespeare has so carefully prepared for the future collision of Antony and Octavius.

This sense of the future coming to life is powerfully evoked at the end of the play and diminishes the personal tragedy associated with the deaths of Brutus and Cassius. During the course of the action the Roman world has changed. Even without the benefit of historical hindsight the impression created is that the 'dogs of war' have a lot more running to do. The new equilibrium, so recently established, is unstable. This is a brave new world in which there is little room for philosophical considerations. In a play dominated by images of blood, hunting, metal and space or room, there is a sudden contraction. The visual image dominating the closing phase of the play, which sees the death of young Cato on the battlefield and several suicides, is the sword. The arena for civil conflict in *Julius Caesar* is the city itself. Whereas the Rome of Julius Caesar could still accommodate the antagonistic watchfulness of Brutus and Cassius, but where Marullus and Flavius are 'put to silence' for removing scarves from Caesar's images, the Rome of the triumvirate has already produced a bloodbath and is in the hands of vigorous politicians for whom even the Roman empire will prove too small.

· 4 ·

Style: Words, Actions and Meanings

One of the play's many distinctive features is its style. John Velz has argued that: 'The most striking of the Roman plays for its style is *Julius Caesar*, though criticism has never done it full justice.' Pointing to the inadequacy of a critical tradition extending from Samuel Johnson, Velz maintains that: 'What is most "Roman" about *Caesar*, however, is not its linguistic leanness, but its oratorical mode . . . the play is filled with the solemnity and the intensity of public utterance.'[1] Recognition of the play's oratorical and formal qualities, however, led distinguished critics such as Mark Van Doren to emphasise this aspect of the play's style to the exclusion of other significant stylistic elements. He shrewdly drew attention to the significance of rhetorical questions in the play and the striking abundance of monosyllables; pointing out that: 'No play of Shakespeare's has so many, so superbly used . . . there may be in one place as many as thirty monosyllables together', so that the effect created by the speaker is of 'artlessness, of sincerity that only speaks right on'. Even so, Van Doren describes the play as 'more rhetoric than poetry', claiming that the characters 'all have something of the statue in them', and even suggesting that '*Julius Caesar* is least notable among Shakespeare's better plays for the distinctions of its speech. All of its persons tend to talk alike.'[2] In sharp contrast Muriel Bradbrook suggests that 'everywhere in this play, the style is the man. . . . All exemplify the art of showing in evolution thought and feelings "as they rise in the mind".[3]

There has been a gradual movement, therefore, towards a recognition of a verbal ease and fluency which counterbalance the play's formal, public quality. A recent editor of the play, who refers aptly to its style as 'lucid and vigorous', has provided an excellent summary of its richly varied verbal texture:

the play is often discussed as if it were formal and deliberate in its speech styles whereas hardly a line lacks temperamental nuance . . . while [Brutus] and Cassius quarrel every word rings with acrimony or distress. The wide range of expressive styles should dispel any idea that Shakespeare sacrificed dramatic idiosyncrasy to *Romanitas*. Everyone speaks a living idiom. . . .

there is much also of vivid picture and stimulating image. Little is abstract or generalized; Shakespeare abounds in sensory effects. . . . Human moods, behaviour, and bodily or facial expression are flashed on the mind's eye. . . .

Within its prevalent clarity the play is strikingly picturesque. Time is made real, the historic past by vivid reminiscence, the present and future by frequent intimations – hours, days, dates, the Ides of March, clocks striking, appointments. . . . There are climatic and atmospheric colourings. . . .

to limit the play to an ordered dignity is to ignore its throbbing pulse, its variegated colour.[4]

An acute awareness of the subtlety of Shakespeare's rhetorical control, his generation of a feeling of movement, excitement and tension, is effectively elucidated by Charles and Michelle Martindale. Commenting on Marullus' chastisement of the plebeians in the opening scene of the play (I.i.32–55) they provide the following analysis:

Here we have the syntactical and rhetorical control, the fire and variety of movement, which we find in Cicero's speeches. Shakespeare obviously noticed for himself, or had pointed out to him at school, the fondness of Latin prose-writers, including Cicero, for the *Tricolon crescendo*: 'You blocks, you stones, you worse than senseless things' (cf. the three questions in 32–34 and again in 48–50, the latter with anaphora of 'And

do you now', and the three clauses with imperatives in 53–55, the
first two carefully balanced structurally). There are rhetorical questions,
apostrophes and exclamations (in 36 with anaphora of 'you' and
balance between 'hard hearts' and 'cruel men'), personification (Tiber
trembling) and a careful variation in the length and impact of sentences.
In 37ff. there is a relentless rhetorical build-up from 'walls' to 'chimney
pots', and on several occasions a special emphasis falls on the last word
in the sentence, for example, 'Pompey's blood' (which contradicts the
sense of triumph) or 'ingratitude', a climactic point which ends the
speech. The language, like Cicero's, generally employs common words,
here seasoned by three elegant Latinisms ('replication', 'concave',
'intermit') in contrast to the overall simplicity of diction. . . . This, we
may feel, is how a Roman orator might speak if he spoke in English.[5]

These comments provide a valuable counterbalance to the conception that
the play is stylistically frigid. The self-conscious nature of this Roman
world is reflected in every word and action. Yet it is not a static world, it
vibrates with human activity and individual sentiment: Cassius cannot
prevent personal malice showing through his ostensibly political attack on
Caesar; Mark Antony, having manipulated the crowd, feels free to utter his
savagely irresponsible:

> Mischief, thou art afoot,
> Take thou what course thou wilt!
>
> (III.ii.262–3)

Likewise, in his colloquy with Octavius after the assassination, he speaks
like a lout. His silver tongue and tender passions have been left in the
Forum. Public pressures and personal anguish exert their influence on
Brutus and Cassius; in the quarrel scene they speak like squabbling
children. Just as logic cannot hold its course – as a Stoic, Brutus is opposed
in principle to suicide yet he determines on that very course of action –
neither do these Romans confine themselves to a controlled formality.
Indeed, that is only one of their aspirations – and it has to compete with
other values which require different expressive modes. The play exhibits
tensions between restraint and passion, gentleness and violence – something clearly recognised and vigorously expressed by G. Wilson Knight:

> The human element in *Julius Caesar* is charged highly with a general
> eroticism. All the people are 'lovers'. This love is emotional, fiery, but
> not exactly sexual, not physically passionate: even Portia and Brutus love

with a gentle companionship rather than any passion. Though the stage be set for an action 'most bloody, fiery, and most terrible', though the action be fine, spirited, and adventurous, and noble blood be magnificently spilt in the third act, yet the human element is often one of gentle sentiment, melting hearts, tears, and the soft fire of love. . . . The word 'lover' is strangely emphatic, sometimes meaning little more than 'friend', but always helping to build a general atmosphere of comradeship and affection. . . . Softness of 'heart' is always a virtue in this play of emotions, especially love. 'O I could weep', says Cassius, 'my spirit from mine eyes' (iv.iii.99). Brutus owes 'more tears' to the dead Cassius than those present shall see him 'pay' (v.iii.101). At the last Brutus ends his long pilgrimage of honour in tears:

> Now is that noble vessel full of grief,
> That it runs over even at his eyes.
>   (v.v.13)

So rich is this play in emotion. It is suffused by a soft sympathy, an interflow of gentle love, sympathetic sorrow.[6]

Yet set against this warm, gentle, emotional, spiritually harmonious strain (symbolised by Lucius' music) is the violence, manifest in the blood imagery and realised physically in the assassination, in the storm, which is again literal, and in animal imagery. There is also the metal/mettle association which finds expression in daggers and swords on the one hand and 'richest alchemy' on the other, by which the conspirators believe Brutus' reputation can transform murder into an act of public service.

Indeed, when it comes to the matter of killing, contrasting attitudes are reflected in differing modes of expression. Brutus justifies and de-brutalises the murder of Caesar by euphemistically transforming it into sacrifice; for Mark Antony the same action constitutes butchery. The proposed killing of Antony is for Cassius a simple, necessary concomitant of the assassination of Caesar, whereas for Brutus it constitutes a senseless violation which he opposes by means of unconvincing arguments and dubious metaphors ('For Antony is but a limb of Caesar' (ii.i.162–5)). Whereas the use of imagery ought to be a source of clarification, in this play it often becomes a source of obfuscation – most obviously in Brutus' orchard soliloquy and again through use of his aphoristic simile ('There is a tide in the affairs of men' (iv.iii.217–20)) as a means to justify fighting at Philippi. Regarding the latter, however, Bradbrook makes the telling point that:

Implicit in such a passage is the denial of perhaps a thousand years of determinism, in which man saw himself as helplessly bound to the wheel of Fortune, the great wheel of the universe, on which every human creature may rise only to fall again.[7]

Shakespeare's encouragement of a critical attitude towards the relationship between expression and action, metaphor and logic, extends outwards to the relationship between event and symbol. At the heart of the play is the contrasting way in which physical phenomena are described and interpreted. The storm experienced and described by Casca carries him to the brink of hysteria, while Cassius achieves a kind of ecstasy under the stimulus of the tempest and his excited anticipation of the assassination. Meanwhile the sceptically detached Cicero delivers himself of a sentiment which could be used as an epigram for the play:

Indeed, it is a strange-disposed time:
But men may construe things, after their fashion,
Clean from the purpose of the things themselves.
                                    (i.iii.33–5)

Brutus reflects on the pyrotechnics only to the extent that he is able to save on candles:

The exhalations whizzing in the air
Give so much light that I may read by them.
                                    (ii.i.44–5)

This issue is discussed with great thoroughness by James R. Siemon, who comments on the way in which the dramatist compels the audience to analyse the conflicting interpretations of characters and events which appear before them. Commenting on the passage from Plutarch which describes the strange happenings preceding Caesar's death, Siemon suggests:

the distinctiveness of Shakespeare's treatment of them lies in the way the play insistently couples the portents with disagreement about their meaning. It is as if Shakespeare had taken the passage from Plutarch and attempted to make it as theatrically impressive and convincing as possible, but had also decided to insist upon the ambiguities resonant in Plutarch's 'perhappes', his 'were sayd to be seene', and his interrogative syntax.[8]

Both historian and dramatist are conscious of the human tendency to give meaning to unusual physical events; to perceive such things as comments by the gods or as premonitions. Thus men interpret events according to their predilections, both through such expressive means as metaphor and by transmuting physical phenomena to the hieroglyphics of the temporal world. An integral feature of this language–event nexus is the verbal patterning which specifically underlines the peculiar relationship between word, gesture and deed. The power that resides in words is continually highlighted and the marriage between word, gesture and deed is given special emphasis. In the opening scene, the plebeians who formerly made 'an universal shout' for Pompey are instructed 'fall upon your knees' as penance for the 'ingratitude' shown in celebrating Caesar's victory over Pompey's sons. The cry of the Soothsayer momentarily produces silence and commands Caesar's attention, but his are the first words of many to be dismissed by Caesar as he weaves his way past an obstacle course of warnings to his assassination. Artemidorus muses as he prepares to deliver his 'petition': 'If thou read this, O Caesar, thou may'st live' (ii.iii.13). He implores Caesar to read the letter (pleading four times) (iii.i.3–9). Caesar has only to take the scroll and read a few words to survive. The warnings of the augurers and the pleas of Calphurnia (on her knees) initially have an effect on Caesar – 'tell them that I will not come to-day' (ii.ii.62) – but they are countered by Decius Brutus' reinterpretation of Calphurnia's dream and promise of a crown. The emphatic 'tell them that I will not come to-day' is subject, therefore, to a striking reversal: 'Give me my robe, for I will go' (ii.ii.107). Neither gesture nor words can keep Caesar from the Senate house, or persuade him to repeal the banishment of Publius Cimber. Feigned pleading gives way to real action with Casca's stark inversion: 'Speak hands for me!' (iii.i.76). This violent action produces chaos as: 'Men, wives, and children stare, cry out, and run,/As it were doomesday.' The conspirators attempt to gain control by the gesture of bathing their hands in Caesar's blood and proceeding to the market-place in accordance with Brutus' injunction:

And waving our red weapons o'er our heads,
Let's all cry, 'Peace, freedom, and liberty!'
(iii.i.97–110)

The incongruity between the visual reality and the abstract slogan never strikes the conspirators. The breakdown in the word–action relationship signalled by Casca's 'Speak hands for me!' is now complete and is further signified in the Casca–Brutus view that the assassins are 'Caesar's friends, that have abridg'd/His time of fearing death' (iii.i.104–5). The absurdity of this declaration (for the audience) is compounded because Caesar has already made explicit that such a fear is incomprehensible to him (ii.ii.34–7). Given this blindness to the true nature of the relationship between gesture and language (bloodied weapons and cries of freedom) it is not surprising that Brutus later employs an abstract formula for making murder an act of compassion (virtually removing the element of the physical):

> And pity to the general wrong of Rome –
> As fire drives out fire, so pity pity –
> Hath done this deed on Caesar.
> (iii.i.170–2)

Brutus, in his orchard soliloquy, has confessed to the impact of Cassius' words upon him:

> Since Cassius first did whet me against Caesar,
> I have not slept.
> Between the acting of a dreadful thing
> And the first motion, all the interim is
> Like a phantasma, or a hideous dream:
> The genius and the mortal instruments
> Are then in council; and the state of man,
> Like to a little kingdom, suffers then
> The nature of an insurrection.
> (ii.i.61–9)

But the action of the assassination does not release him from internal tension. He never seems totally convinced of the rightness of the action. In contrast, Mark Antony manifests no sign of internal doubts and is absolutely clear-eyed about the power of language and gesture. Despite being genuinely moved by Caesar's death, he plots his course with calculated guile, cynically taking the bloodied hands of the assassins in apparent friendship while mentally placing them on a death list. To Antony, Caesar's wounds 'like dumb mouths do ope their ruby lips,/To beg the voice and utterance of my tongue' (iii.i.260–72). His response is to turn his hostile audience – ''Twere best he speak no harm of Brutus here!' (iii.ii.70) – into a frantic mob. The plebeians who initially deny him a respectful hearing are manipulated into pleading 'Read the will!' (iii.ii.149) before completing the process from receipt of the word to action: 'We'll hear him, we'll follow him, we'll die with him' (iii.ii.210). Having fashioned them perfectly to his will, the master of oratory is able to deny he has such power, claiming that the spur to action is the sight of Caesar's wounds: 'But yesterday the word of Caesar might/Have stood against the world' (iii.ii.120–1). Today, the wounds that failed to speak directly for Caesar are made to speak by Antony's words and gestures:

> I come not, friends, to steal away your hearts.
> I am no orator, as Brutus is,
> But (as you know me all) a plain blunt man,
> That love my friend; and that they know full well
> That gave me public leave to speak of him.
> For I have neither wit, nor words, nor worth,
> Action, nor utterance, nor the power of speech
> To stir men's blood; I only speak right on.
> I tell you that which you yourselves do know,
> Show you sweet Caesar's wounds, poor poor dumb mouths,
> And bid them speak for me.
>
> (iii.ii.218–28)

A fascinating exploration of the Forum speeches has been undertaken by Alessandro Serpieri in his paper 'Reading the signs: towards a semiotics of Shakespearean drama'. Serpieri's analysis of Antony's rhetorical techniques is particularly illuminating and is worth quoting at some length:

> The basic axes of his speech are indirect, founded on a continuous game of assertion and negation: he affirms through irony and emphasis in order to negate, while he negates through litotes, through paralepsis and through *detractio*, in order to affirm. . . .
> In addition to the use of irony, the primary rhetorical mode of Antony's utterance is that which employs litotes. The litotic mode is understood as a figure of thought, of word, and of dramatic (and potentially stage) illocution. Litotes of thought pervades the entire oration in its various articulations: he has come to rouse the people in the name of Caesar against the name of Brutus who had acted on behalf of the people; he cannot say so directly, and indeed has to maintain the contrary, but working through upsets in sense he manages to overturn the explicit propositions and reach his ideological and political end. Litotes of word is frequent and very effective: 'I come to bury Caesar, *not* to praise him' (line 76); 'I speak *not* to disprove what Brutus spoke' (102); 'I will *not* do them wrong' (line 127), etc. . . . Negation is always used by way of

enticement, and so is always, basically, a litotes, a figure which transmits the very sense that it claims to hide.

It is a figure which has, moreover, an immediate dramatic and theatrical import. At a certain point, Antony arranges the crowd in a circle around Caesar's body and calls attention to Caesar's corpse covered by the toga (lines 171–99). But for almost all his speech, he stresses *not* the massacred body of Caesar, which in fact he does not uncover, but the leader's torn and bloody toga, an emblem at once of rank and of suffering. The toga is a double sign on which Antony can work, appealing to all the emotional registers: the pathetic (the first evening he saw him wear it), the epic (that evening was the eve of the great victory against the Nervii), the blasphemous (the hole caused by the wretched blade of Brutus, 'Caesar's angel'), the stoical (Caesar, destroyed by Brutus's ingratitude, covered his face with the same toga). At once sign and simulacrum, the toga unleashes all the emotions, and the crowd weeps. But at the end, in an extraordinary *coup de théâtre*, Antony benevolently rebukes the people for having let themselves be moved *only* by Caesar's 'vesture', by a mere simulacrum, and then uncovers the massacred *referent* itself:

> Kind souls, what weep you when you but behold
> Our Caesar's vesture wounded? Look you here!
> Here is himself, marr'd, as you see, with traitors.
>   (iii.ii.197–9)

Even this move, exquisitely dramatic as it is, falls under the rubric of litotes: negating or suspending in order to affirm; working on the emotions through a minor point in order to unleash them through the major point; allowing only a part of the sense or evidence to filter through, precisely so that the meaning may burst out because of the blocking of a direct flow, or, as here, of a direct reference to the 'object'. Everything has to be rendered indirect, oblique.[9]

The word, then, allied with the gesture is all powerful in precipitating the deed. Often, in this play, it is the words or noises coming from off-stage that have a critical effect. The most striking example of this is the influence exerted on Brutus who fears that the shouts from off-stage are for the crowning of Caesar. Those shouts provide a vital ingredient for Cassius' otherwise incomplete process of persuasion. Indeed, at the end of his harangue Cassius is grateful to settle for a partial success:

> I am glad
> That my weak words have struck but thus much show
> Of fire from Brutus.
>
> (I.ii.173–5)

The fire is further kindled, of course, by Casca's wonderfully wrought, partial account of Caesar rejecting the crown. Casca's own theatrical talents are fully engaged when describing those of Caesar, who so manipulated the crowd that 'the rabblement hooted, and clapp'd their chopt hands, and threw up their sweaty night-caps' (I.ii.240–2). The interrogation of Casca by Brutus and Cassius, and Casca's description of the crown-offering, is structured around the principle of words and the response to them in the form of words or gestures. Casca interprets the performance, but for all his seemingly off-hand indifference, he delineates every movement with the utmost precision. It is pure theatre with every word and gesture finely calculated. Finally, his casually delivered last piece of news points out the nature of the relationship between words and deeds in the political sphere: Marullus and Flavius 'for *pulling scarfs off Caesar's images* are *put to silence*' (I.ii.282–3). Having access to neither words nor deeds, they are now politically impotent. In the context of this description of political theatre, the expression 'put to silence' gathers enormous potency.

Furthermore, Cassius' description of his swimming contest with Caesar is designed to point out the discrepancy between Caesar's confident challenge and his inadequate physical response. It is this dichotomy between the assumed stature and the reality which constitutes the moral of Cassius' description of Caesar's epileptic fit:

> Ay, and *that tongue of his*, that bade the Romans
> *mark him and write his speeches in their books*,
> Alas it *cried*, 'Give me some drink, Titinius,'
> *As a sick girl.*
>
> (I.ii.124–7)

For Cassius there is something inherently ludicrous about Caesar's presumption that his words should be recorded for posterity and then feebly calling for assistance. Nicholas Brooke makes the observation that this contrast constitutes part of the dominant image pattern of the play:

[a] continual juxtapostition of heroic valuation with crude physical characteristics – strength in swimming, sick girl, huge legs, fat men, deaf

ear: these are merely men, playing out a noble action ('mmortal Caesar) which is also a grotesque (almost Falstaffian) comedy: an uncomfortable reflection.[10]

Telling though this is, Norman Sanders is surely correct when he claims that:

> we *hear* the recital of the epileptic sick girl and the spent swimmer calling out for aid, but it is the god whose 'tongue . . . bade the Romans/Mark him and write his speeches in their books', and who bestrides the world like a Colossus, that catches the imagination.[11]

Nevertheless, the deflating undercurrent noted by Brooke is undoubtedly present and at the very least operates at a subconscious level. As Bullough expresses it: 'With *Julius Caesar*, one feels, Shakespeare was on the way towards the denigration of heroic and romantic myth which exposed the weaknesses of Greeks and Trojans alike in *Troilus and Cressida*.'[12] Or as Bullman has more recently commented, Shakespeare's 'treatment of heroic conventions seems detached, ironic, even satirical'.[13]

Another facet of this connection between word and deed is exhibited by Caius Ligarius. Sick though he is, it takes but a word from Brutus to make him capable of action:

> Now bid me run,
> And I will strive with things impossible
> (ii.i.324–5)

Brutus' failure, however, to respond appropriately to Decius' hint – 'Shall no man else be touch'd but only Caesar?' (ii.i.154) – is crucial, especially as he later disregards Cassius' warning about the potential danger of Antony's words:

> Brutus, a word with you.
> [*Aside.*] You know not what you do. Do not consent
> That Antony speak in his funeral.
> (iii.i.231–3)

This complex fabric of connections between words, gestures and deeds is most clearly underlined and marvellously bought out in the parley that precedes the battle:

Bru.	*Words* before *blows*: is it so, countrymen?
Oct.	Not that we *love words better*, as you do.
Bru.	*Good words* are better than *bad strokes*, Octavius.
Ant.	In your *bad strokes*, Brutus, you give *good words*;
	Witness the *hole you made in Caesar's heart*,
	Crying, '*Long live! Hail*, Caesar!'
Cas.	Antony,
	The posture of your *blows* are yet unknown;
	But for your *words*, they rob the Hybla bees,
	And leave them honeyless.
Ant.	Not *stingless* too.
Bru.	O yes, and *soundless* too;
	For you have stol'n their *buzzing*, Antony,
	And very wisely *threat* before you *sting*.
Ant.	Villains! you did not so when your vile daggers
	Hack'd one another in the sides of Caesar:
	You *show'd your teeth* like apes, and *fawn'd* like hounds,
	And *bow'd* like bondmen, *kissing* Caesar's feet;
	Whilst damned Casca, like a cur, behind
	struck Caesar on the neck. O you flatterers!
Cas.	Flatterers? Now, Brutus, thank yourself.
	This *tongue* had not offended so to-day,
	If Cassius might have rul'd.

(v.i.27–47)

Indeed to the very end of the play there is an emphasis on the decisiveness of the single word. The battle is lost, Titinius says, because 'Brutus gave the word too early' (v.iii.5). Even then victory might have been salvaged except that Pindarus and Cassius misinterpret the shouts that accompany Titinius' welcome. Cato charges into action with the words 'I will proclaim my name about the field' (v.iv.3). Finally, with defeat inevitable, the word–deed connection is forged by Brutus: 'Slaying is the word;/It is a deed in fashion' (v.v.4–5). The action-embodying quality of the word is underlined by Messala, who in preparing to carry the news of Cassius' death to Brutus talks of 'thrusting this report/Into his ears' (v.iii.74–5). Brutus causes horror and dismay among his friends by asking them to aid his suicide. The whispered word is too painful for them. Yet Lucilius is ultimately glad that Brutus has fulfilled his prediction: 'I thank thee, Brutus,/That thou hast prov'd Lucilius saying true' (v.v.58–9).

Closely connected with this word–action paradigm are the significances attaching to hands and hearts. Before taking Brutus' sword for him to run upon Strato says simply: 'Give me your hand first' (v.v.49). As the quarrel between Cassius and Brutus subsides the former says eagerly: 'Give me your hand', to which Brutus responds: 'And my heart too' (iv.iii.116–17). The clasping of hands, however, is not always a gesture of love. Antony asks the conspirators: 'Let each man render me his bloody hand' (iii.i.184), in an act of daring dissimulation, having earlier drawn attention to how their 'purpled hands do reek and smoke' (iii.i.158). Brutus protests, sincerely, that it is a paradox, but for the audience, and Antony too, it is a simple contradiction:

> Though now we must appear bloody and cruel,
> As by our hands and this our present act
> You see we do, yet see you but our hands
> And this the bleeding business they have done.
> Our hearts you see not; they are pitiful;
>
> (iii.i.165–9)

Such abstractions are entirely alien to Antony, merely provoking him to vow: 'Woe to the hand that shed this costly blood!' (iii.i.258). In order to avenge his friend he is willing to contemplate the vision of 'infants quartered with the hands of war' (iii.i.268). Casca offers his hand to Cassius as a seal of contract – 'Hold, my hand' (i.iii.117) – but it is more in his nature to comment sardonically on the simple-minded response of the plebeians who 'clapp'd their chopt hands' (i.ii.241). Nevertheless he fulfils his bond when making the most terrible utterance in the play: 'Speak hands for me!' (iii.i.76).

More pervasive even than the references to hands are those to hearts, and again the association is not always with love and tenderness. Caesar, perceiving Cassius as a malcontent, comments: 'Such men as he be never at heart's ease' (i.ii.205). Casca pours scorn on the plebeians for their response to Caesar when they 'forgave him with all their hearts' (i.ii.270) and he recognises a special regard for Brutus who 'sits high in all the people's hearts' (i.iii.157). Caius Ligarius promises to follow Brutus with 'a heart new-fir'd' (ii.i.332). Brutus assures Portia that she is: 'As dear to me as are the ruddy drops/That visit my sad heart' (ii.i.289–90), before promising to reveal to her the 'secrets of my heart' (ii.i.306). Portia, in turn, muses sorrowfully: 'how weak a thing/The heart of woman is!' (ii.iv.39–40). Metellus Cimber cynically claims to place before Caesar: 'An humble heart' (iii.i.35), and Artemidorus reflects: 'My heart laments that virtue cannot live/Out of the teeth of emulation' (ii.iii.11–12). Meanwhile Brutus grieves that the ceremony of wine-taking with Caesar does not betoken genuine friendship – 'The heart of Brutus earns to think upon' (II.ii.129). The assassination over, Cassius proposes that the conspirators follow Brutus in procession: 'With the most boldest and best hearts of Rome' (III.i.121). Brutus offers Antony 'hearts/Of brothers' temper' (III.i.174–5); Antony grieves over Caesar's body: 'And this indeed, O world, the heart of thee' (III.i.208), and in his funeral oration he has to pause, he says, because: 'My heart is in the coffin there with Caesar' (III.ii.108). He gathers himself to describe the moment when Caesar recognised Brutus' betrayal: 'then burst his mighty heart' (III.ii.188). Yet, he promises his audience: 'I come not, friends, to steal away your hearts' (III.ii.218). It is ironic that the most coolly calculating character in the play, Octavius Caesar, cautions Antony with the words: 'And some that smile have in their hearts, I fear,/Millions of mischiefs' (IV.i.50–1). Brutus, during his quarrel with Cassius insists:

> I had rather coin my heart,
> And drop my blood for drachmas, than to wring
> From the hard hands of peasants their vile trash.
> (IV.iii.72–4)

Under the pressure of Brutus' onslaught Cassius claims that 'Brutus hath riv'd my heart' and goes on to offer 'a heart/Dearer than Pluto's mine, richer than gold'. The rift healed, Cassius expresses his joy: 'My heart is thirsty for that noble pledge' (IV.iii.84–159). Titinius, on discovering his dead friend, Cassius, expresses his grief with the words: 'O my heart!' (V.iii.58).

Like the heart – the symbol of tenderness – the word love runs like a leitmotif through the play. The love shared by Brutus and Caesar is one of the play's enigmas. Brutus confesses to Cassius: 'Yet I love him well' (I.ii.81), while Cassius sorrows that Caesar 'loves Brutus' (I.ii.310), then later protests to his friend: 'When thou didst hate him worst, thou lov'dst him better/Than ever thou lov'dst Cassius' (IV.iii.105–6). Brutus protests to the crowd that his killing of Caesar was an act of personal sacrifice to a greater good: 'Not that I loved Caesar less, but that I love Rome more'; acknowledging that he was loved in turn Brutus claims: 'As Caesar loved me, I weep for him', before concluding: 'I slew my best lover for the good of Rome' (III.ii.22–46). Antony uses that love as a weapon against Brutus: 'Judge, O you gods, how dearly Caesar lov'd him' (III.ii.184). Entirely different in feeling is Antony's avowal over the body of his friend and mentor: 'That I did love thee, Caesar, O, 'tis true!' (III.i.194). At the other extreme is Antony's cynical message to Brutus that he 'shall not love Caesar

dead/So well as Brutus living' (III.i.133–4). Cassius, who understands love
in the direct way that Brutus does not, fears Antony: 'For in the ingrafted
love he bears to Caesar' (II.i.184). The man who cautions Brutus: 'Do not
presume too much upon my love', protests: 'You do not love me', before
warmly accepting Brutus' reassurance with the words: 'I cannot drink too
much of Brutus' love' (IV.iii.63–161). As the final battle approaches
Cassius says to Brutus: 'The gods to-day stand friendly, that we may,/
Lovers in peace, lead on our days to age!' (V.i.94–5). Perhaps the complete
antithesis to this deep well-spring of human affection is the relationship
between Decius Brutus and Caesar. Decius, in the very process of drawing
Caesar to his death, proclaims 'my dear dear love', insisting: 'And reason to
my love is liable' (II.ii.102–4).

   Closely associated with these declarations of love is the concept of value
which finds expression in several places in the play. Cassius claims that he
has kept from Brutus: 'Thoughts of great value, worthy cogitations', before
proceeding to reveal Brutus' 'hidden worthiness' (I.ii.49, 56). Casca and
Cassius have an important exchange which also focuses on Brutus' worth
and employs the metal imagery of the play:

Casca	His countenance, like richest alchemy,
	Will change to virtue and to worthiness.
Cas.	Him and his worth and our great need of him
	You have right well conceited.

(I.iii.159–62)

Likewise Metullus Cimber recognises the value of Cicero to the conspiracy:

for his silver hairs
Will purchase us a good opinion,
And buy men's voices to commend our deeds.
(II.i.143–5)

Antony tells the assassins that their swords are 'made rich/With the most
noble blood of all this world' (III.i.155–6). Brutus confides to his colleagues
surrounding the body of Cassius: 'I owe more tears/To this dead man than
you shall see me pay' (V.iii.101–2), while Antony confirms that in Lucilius
they have: 'A prize no less in worth' than Brutus (V.iv.27).

   Another aspect of verbal and conceptual association is verbal patterning.
A rhetorical device which Shakespeare uses to great effect in this play
is verbal symmetry (especially a combination of anaphora, parison and
isocolon). The device of symmetrical construction is employed, in conjunction with questions, in Marullus' merciless harangue of the people:

And do you now put on your best attire?
And do you now cull out a holiday?
And do you now strew flowers in his way,
That comes in triumph over Pompey's blood?
(I.i.48–51)

This unrelenting quality, sauced with irony, is also present in Cassius'
mockery of Casca's fear of the storm:

Why all these fires, why all these gliding ghosts,
Why birds and beasts from quality and kind,
Why old men, fools, and children calculate,
Why all these things change from their ordinance,
(I.iii.63–6)

It is Cassius again in colloquy with Casca, who engages in this verbal
structure:

Therein, ye gods, you make the weak most strong;
Therein, ye gods, you tyrants do defeat.
Nor stony tower, nor walls of beaten brass,
Nor airless dungeon, nor strong links of iron,
. . .
Poor man! I know he would not be a wolf,
But that he sees the Romans are but sheep;
He were no lion, were not Romans hinds.
(I.iii.91–106)

The emotional effect of verbal symmetry is quite different in Portia's
plaintive appeal to Brutus, but the powerfully insistent quality inherent in
this rhetorical figure is equally apparent:

I grant I am a woman; but withal
A woman that Lord Brutus took to wife;
I grant I am a woman; but withal
A woman well reputed, Cato's daughter.
(II.i.292–5)

The substance of this scene in which Portia pleads with Brutus to open
his heart to her is provided by Plutarch. Shakespeare heightens the account
not only by introducing a wider vocabulary and more effective diction, but

by injecting a greater sense of urgency into Portia's appeal. In particular Shakespeare uses a series of rhetorical questions with a play on the words 'sick', 'by', 'you', 'yours' and 'vows':

Is Brutus sick, and is it physical
To walk unbraced and suck up the humours
Of the dank morning? What, is Brutus sick?
And will he steal out of his wholesome bed
To dare the vile contagion of the night,
And tempt the rheumy and unpurged air
To add unto his sickness? No, my Brutus;
You have some sick offence within your mind,
Which, by the right and virtue of my place,
I ought to know of; and, upon my knees,
I charm you, by my once commended beauty,
By all your vows of love, and that great vow
Which did incorporate and make us one,
That you unfold to me, your self, your half,
Why you are heavy,

(ii.i.261–75)

As the emotional temperature rises Portia kneels before Brutus and continues her plea with great force and dignity:

Bru.   Kneel not, gentle Portia.
Por.   I should not need, if you were gentle Brutus.
      Within the bond of marriage, tell me, Brutus,
      Is it excepted I should know no secrets
      That appertain to you? Am I your self
      But, as it were, in sort or limitation,
      To keep with you at meals, comfort your bed,
      And talk to you sometimes? Dwell I but in the suburbs
      Of your good pleasure? If it be no more,
      Portia is Brutus' harlot, not his wife.
Bru.   You are my true and honourable wife,
      As dear to me as are the ruddy drops
      That visit my sad heart.

(ii.i.278–90)

Once more questions are used as the key structural element. Shakespeare adopts the word 'harlot' from his source but he intensifies its power by prefacing it with the wonderfully effective phrase: 'Dwell I but in the suburbs/Of your good pleasure?' There is not so much as a hint in the source material to give Shakespeare even the embryo of Brutus' moving reply – a response that elevates him in the mind of the audience. Finally, this figure is used to produce a spiritual coalescing in the farewell between Brutus and Cassius. As their antagonisms are totally dissolved, harmony is reflected in verbal symmetry:

> *Bru.* For ever, and for ever, farewell, Cassius.
> If we do meet again, why, we shall smile;
> If not, why then this parting was well made.
> *Cas.* For ever, and for ever, farewell, Brutus.
> If we do meet again, we'll smile indeed;
> If not, 'tis true this parting was well made.
> (v.i.117–22)

The numerous references to hands, hearts, knees, heels, stomach, teeth, bowels, neck, tongues, eyes, brows and the all-pervasive blood lend the play a tremendous physicality. Cassius asks: 'Upon what meat doth this our Caesar feed,/That he is grown so great?', while Cassius, himself, is described as having 'a lean and hungry look' (i.ii.147–8, 191). Indeed, a great deal of the sense of human physicality and energy is generated by Cassius. In asserting his integrity to Brutus, he protests:

> if you know
> That I do fawn on men and hug them hard,
> And after scandal them; . . .
> . . .
> then hold me dangerous.
> (i.ii.73–7)

Likewise, in his wonderful description of his swimming contest with Caesar, we experience human will and muscle contending with the elemental forces of nature:

> The torrent roar'd, and we did buffet it
> With lusty sinews, throwing it aside
> And stemming it with hearts of controversy
> (i.ii.106–8)

These elemental forces are let loose in the storm when 'all the sway of earth/Shakes like a thing unfirm?' (i.iii.3–4). Caesar partakes of these

powerful forces of nature and is 'prodigious grown' (i.iii.77). Moreover, 'he
doth bestride the narrow world/Like a Colossus' (i.ii.133–4). He is also an
eagle or a falcon who seeks to 'soar above the view of men/And keep us all
in servile fearfulness' (i.i.74–5). These images all point to the unnatural in
Julius Caesar: he seeks to overwhelm by his godlike singularity. This is the
thrust of Cassius' argument in his enticement of Brutus:

> When could they say, till now, that talk'd of Rome,
> That her wide walks encompass'd but one man?
>   (i.ii.152–3)

That this is no mere posture is revealed in his outburst to Casca:

>   for Romans now
> Have thews and limbs like to their ancestors;
> But, woe the while! our fathers' minds are dead,
>
>   (i.iii.80–2)

Brents Stirling's comments on the role of ceremony have already been
mentioned, but this argument has recently been developed by Alan Hager,
who suggests that 'human sacrifice is on everyone's lips in this play'.[14] As
well as this element of ceremony or ritual, however, there are a number of
parallel ritual reversals. At the opening of the play Caesar's images are
decorated with diadems or festival adornments which Marullus and Flavius
remove or 'disrobe'. At the opening of the chase in the second scene of the
play Caesar insists 'leave no ceremony out' (i.ii.11). But after the fiasco
of the crown-offering by Antony, and Caesar's untimely collapse, the
'chidden train' that returns signifies a broken ritual. Once Brutus is
committed to the assassination, Cassius immediately proposes the taking of
a solemn oath. Brutus rejects this ceremony only to replace it with the
suggestion that the assassination itself will be a ritualistic killing. Both
Portia and Calphurnia kneel before their husbands in an endeavour to
influence them. Calphurnia (implicitly) and Decius (explicitly) interpret
her terrible dream. Caesar chooses to ignore the bad omen. The reality,
witnessed by the audience, chillingly accords with Calphurnia's literal
interpretation. However, by the end of the play Caesar achieves the
mythological status of demi-god, thereby fulfilling Decius' (duplicitous)
metaphorical prediction. Again there is a parallel between the prostration
of Metellus Cimber before Caesar in a posture of false supplication, and
Antony's servant repeating the gesture before the conspirators, and having
the same intention to deceive. Brutus insists that Antony be allowed to

speak at Caesar's funeral so that he shall: 'Have all true rites and lawful ceremonies' (III.i.241), but Antony turns the ceremony into political action which finally explodes into irrational violence. Technically, distinctions can be made between the ceremonial or ritualistic quality of these gestures, but in terms of stage effects they possess remarkable affinities and form part of the verbal–visual patterning of the play, thereby contributing to its distinctive stylistic structure.[15] Gunter Walch has pointed out that: 'Passages probing the differences between "seeming", "appearing", "acting", "fashioning", "construing", and the world of reality occur thirty-five times in the text.'[16]

The connections between acting, ceremony and fashioning have recently been highlighted by John Drakakis, who develops his argument along the following lines:

In his instruction to Marullus to 'Disrobe the images,/If you do find them decked with ceremonies' (I.i.64–5), Flavius initiates a deconstruction of the very representations which are a constitutive element of Caesar's success. They are the signifying practices which both position Caesar 'above the view of men', at the same time as they reinforce the social hierarchy by keeping 'us all in servile fearfulness' (I.i.74–5). The following scene firmly inscribes Caesar in the process of 'ceremony' both as a producer and an actor, of whom Antony can say: 'When Caesar says "Do this" it is perform'd.' (I.ii.12), and who insists upon a complete performance: 'Set on and leave no ceremony out.' (I.ii.13). By contrast, Brutus admits, 'I am not gamesome;' (I.ii.30), although this anti-festive expression is quickly belied by a tacit admission of consummate acting: 'If I have veiled my look,/I turn the trouble of my countenance/Merely upon myself.' (I.ii.39–41); and similarly, the Cassius who eschews ritual but articulates his political desires through its language, is later affirmed by Caesar as an enemy of theatrical performance: 'He loves no plays,' (I.ii.204). . . .
Resistant though the conspirators are to the Caesarian control of institutions and meanings, they formulate a strategy of temporary release and restraint which parallels the *ideological* usage of festivity, extending the potential for containment to the affective power of tragic form itself. These concerns are concentrated with remarkable economy in Brutus's appeal to his fellow conspirators: 'And let our hearts, as subtle masters do,/Stir up their servants to an act of rage,/And after seem to chide 'em.' (II.i.175–7). From this point on the talk is of 'fashioning', of manufacturing, and hence of historicizing, truth, and inevitably, of theatrical representation. The fully-fashioned Brutus will

now undertake to 'fashion' Caius Ligarius (II.i.219). . . . Also Cassius's bid to revive Roman self-presence with his exhortation to the conspirators to 'Show yourselves true Romans' (II.i.222) is expanded by the one character whose 'countenance' is endowed with transformative power: 'let not our looks put on our purposes;/But bear it as our Roman actors do,/With untired spirits and formal constancy' (II.i.224–6). Here theatrical representation is neither illusion nor self-delusion, rather it is the ground upon which the symbols of authority are contested.[17]

Barbara J. Baines has also directed attention to the process of fashioning and the play's insistence on the connection between the political and the theatrical, the re-presentation of events, and closely connected with these, the instabilities of language:

> A dramatization of the art of rhetoric, *Julius Caesar* depicts the fashioning of political reality through speech. Indeed, no other work of the Renaissance demonstrates more forcefully the power of words to shape the course of history. The poet's power to fashion through words a world on the stage serves here as a paradigm for the politician's power to shape the course of political events. . . . As the various politicians of the play attempt to displace the poet by appropriating his art, they become subject to the instabilities of language, and thus paradoxically they reveal that power, political as well as poetic, is provisional – achieved by and subject to revision. . . . At the end of the play, we as readers are no closer than the characters to an understanding of 'the things themselves'. Because *Julius Caesar* insists on the re-visioning that language compels, the play calls into doubt the epistemological reliability of language. Irony and uncertainty are the effects of increased awareness of the gap between intent and deed, between word and referent. What we do understand is that our comprehension of reality is a subjectivist fashioning through suspect words and that what is fashioned by the word is always subject to revision.[18]

Even more recently Thomas Healy has developed another element of the language-politics-theatre nexus. Examining Brutus' orchard soliloquy he redirects the focus away from interior psychological analysis:

> This is commonly perceived as an interior debate as Brutus tries to decide what should be done. But it hardly seems a dramatic articulation of character. As the language with its repeated serpent imagery suggests, the speech is concerned with finding a public representation of the

grounds for killing Caesar. Brutus is certain of what he intends as the speech opens: 'It must be by his death.' What he is concerned with is the discovery of the right formulation to 'fashion it thus', a means of presentation that will persuade an audience that Caesar needed to die and was killed by actions undertaken in the public rather than in a private interest. What Caesar is will have to be re-presented by Brutus: 'since the quarrel will bear no colour for the thing he is'. Brutus's choice of Caesar as the serpent's egg is selected as the suitable formulation of the equation between Caesar and serpents that Brutus has been toying with throughout. The speech is a good example of formal rhetorical argument by analogy rather than logic. It shows Brutus adept in the use of rhetoric and looking forward to his public defence of Caesar's assassination to the Roman crowd. The speech does not create a distance between the public arguments used and the imagined private moments. Brutus's self is one founded on his public and not his private identity. Brutus and the other characters can be presented as representatives of political actions: the play explores the lack of distance between private and public relations. All the characters are fashioning actions through words, so that the quality of both words and actions becomes unsettled, dependent on political expediency.

And he concludes his analysis of the play with another pertinent comment on the implications of the space between contradictory statements, actions or perceptions:

Within *Julius Caesar* Antony's claim at the play's conclusion that 'this was the noblest Roman of them all' is frequently taken as some type of authentic commentary on Brutus and becomes the focus for critical exploration into Brutus's character. Nobility is taken as self-defined, a virtue which right-thinking readers ought to recognise, or a Roman ideal the terms of which the play defines (and sympathises with). But the play may be seen to represent 'Roman nobility' as a highly questionable ideal, a manner of staging oneself within a realm of political theatre. 'Nobility' is not an intrinsic quality, but a publicly defined attribute supported by birth and education (the conspirators and Antony, the play suggests, all went to school togther – I.ii.294–5). What Brutus or any of the characters 'really are' is not the centre of their dramatic interest. The play's interest, rather, is centred on how they act: both what they do and what they say, and the gap between the two.[19]

Julius Caesar, then, is a play characterised by an elusive stylistic quality. Abounding in monosyllables, having a smaller vocabulary than any of the other plays apart from *The Comedy of Errors* and *The Two Gentlemen of Verona*, and almost devoid of the extended metaphors endemic in other Shakespearian plays, it has in the past been lauded for its strictly Roman oratorical quality rather than for its humanly enriching personal elements. It is a play where every word has the individual firmness of a stone. Perhaps, in a way unique to this play, there is a potency which resides in the words themselves, even when untouched by metaphorical colouring. As R. A. Foakes has shown, even names have a symbolic significance: 'The word Caesar had long been used to signify an all-conquering, absolute monarch, and is used in the play with this implication.' He points out that: 'The names of Caesar (211 times), Brutus (130 times) and to a much lesser degree Cassius (69 times) and Antony (68 times) echo through the play, and are frequently used where a pronoun would occur in the other tragedies.' Brutus is associated with honour; Rome and Roman with freedom: 'The conspirators, especially Brutus and Cassius, associate themselves with Rome as the home of truth, honour, liberty and manliness.'[20] Critics have observed how Caesar frequently speaks of himself in the third person, but this trait is by no means confined to the great man. Portia stresses that she is Cato's daughter and the young man who dies in the final battle rushes to his death proclaiming himself the son of Marcus Cato. The past continually exerts a pressure on the present and this is reflected in the frequent references to Pompey the Great (whose name is mentioned ten times – and three times within two dozen lines prior to the assassination).[21] Cassius, in making the comparison between his rescue of Caesar from the Tiber and Aeneas saving his father from the flames of Troy, brings to mind a genuine religious icon: the living, breathing Cassius associates himself directly with his 'great ancestor' and founder of Rome; the past finds expression in the present through the blood of the great Roman family and through the principles which animate Roman society. There is, indeed, everything in a name, as Cinna the poet discovers when he becomes the surrogate victim for Cinna the conspirator.

One of the great ironies of the play is the way in which Mark Antony begins his oration by giving expression to a sentiment which is a persistent theme throughout the play, namely the relationship between 'Brutus' and 'honourable'. This he articulates repeatedly before undermining and finally inverting the equation. Significantly, during his oration, Brutus speaks of himself in the third person, retaining his dignity and distance from the crowd, whereas Antony, 'the plain blunt man', leaves the pulpit to mingle with the crowd, disclaiming any connection with oratory. In many ways the Forum speeches summarise the play's stylistic dualities. Brutus, the detached servant of Rome, seems only to make clear the state of affairs. The speech is pithy, succinct, possessing the incisiveness and precision of a mathematical formula. Antony, the master of oratory, plays on every facet of the crowd's emotions, giving a vivid picture of the noble Julius in his tent 'That day he overcame the Nervii', before presenting the grim theatrical props of 'Our Caesar's vesture wounded' and the mangled body. Here is a great art that conceals art – something seeming to emanate directly from the heart. Shakespeare the dramatist reveals how various devices of rhetoric can be employed in such a way as to give a feeling of naturalism. The proscription scene generates a different cadence: the harsh tones of self-interested politicians ruthlessly arranging events and organising judicial murder in a manner which can best be described as the discourse of everyday life.

Recent criticism of the play points out the rich interpretive possibilities inherent in the words, gestures and deeds – and the subtle tensions that characterise their interconnections. Just as Thomas Healy insists that *Julius Caesar* invites a questioning of such fundamental concepts as nobility, so too does it call for an analysis of fashioning in all its forms: self-images, values, arguments, symbols and rituals – and crucially, interpretation. The characters are self-conscious actors fully aware of their historic roles. But the play is never done. Each re-enactment takes place against the background of a changing social universe so that new actors and new audiences continually reinterpret and refashion. Perhaps, as Barbara J. Baines suggests, Brutus mirrors the unending quest for the achievement of a settled judgement that is never really attainable because of the human propensity to refashion words and actions.[22]

· 5 ·

Conclusion:
'There is a tide in the affairs
of men'

Julius Caesar is a paradoxical play. Simple and complex – critics have found it cold and formal yet intimately personal and moving. The assassination of Julius Caesar had been the subject of vigorous controversy from the time it was perpetrated in 44 BC right up to Shakespeare's own day. If many went to the theatre expecting answers to that great debate, what they encountered was a play which embraced all the recognised historical enigmas with some added for good measure. Discussions of Antony's place in history focused on his association with Cleopatra, yet Shakespeare's character is vividly brought to life in *Julius Caesar*. Charismatic leader and opportunist, he enters the play as Caesar's sycophantic servant, becomes his dynamic avenger but sinks with rapidity into a cynical manipulator. The character who at the start of the action is in the shadow of the great Julius is by the end of it entering the shadow of the uncharismatic Octavius. Cassius, the passionate, jealous, loving man engages the sympathy of the audience through his vigorous language and through his all too human frailties. Guilty of jealousy, guile and malice, he finally attracts a warm response because of his capacity for love and his disillusioned awareness of failure. Ironically Cassius' true opposite is the Caesar who survives rather than the Caesar who dies. Octavius Caesar's icy cold precision, self-containment, assurance and ambition together make up a character who is the complete antithesis of Cassius.

All the characters in this play are powerfully conceived and their personalities sharply delineated. The speakers have their own distinctive vocabulary, inflection and speech rhythm. Part of the distinction of the play resides in this potent individuality of character which bestows on the dialogue vitality and authenticity. The intermingling of the personal and idiosyncratic with a consciousness of political identities gives unique texture to the play. Relatively narrow in its lexical range, and constrained in its metaphorical expression, the language, nevertheless, exploits fully the rhetorical devices at the dramatist's command. The feeling is not of sparseness but of precision. When characters employ metaphors in this play they are generally carried away by them. Brutus' 'serpent's egg', his vision of 'a sacrifice fit for the gods' and his 'tide in the affairs of men' obscure reality rather than clarify it, and the same can be said of Julius Caesar's images of himself as a 'lion' and 'the northern star', not to mention Antony's apostrophe to the 'stricken deer'. Here the image is a false coin and is employed as such by Mark Antony, who can so tellingly refer to Brutus as 'Caesar's angel'.

The play which opens with the noise and turmoil of the crowd celebrating the triumph of Caesar over Pompey's sons closes to the cool tones of Octavius Caesar. The plebeians of Rome exert a decisive influence over events in the Forum scene, but they are destructive rather than creative: the truculent vitality of the cobbler in the opening scene gives way to black humour in the ugly and senseless murder of Cinna the poet (who, incidentally, in his dozen lines reveals an entire personality: fastidious and pedantic, he is totally out of his depth in the company of these violent, uncouth men). Here is the living reality of what Antony lets loose with such relish ('mischief thou art afoot') – it is surpassed in cruelty only by the cold-blooded judicial murders initiated in the proscription scene. These two scenes are characteristic of the play in generating emotional shifts and contrasts. Again the cold cynicism of the proscription scene is contrasted with the full-blooded passion of the quarrel scene. Juxtaposition of the husband-wife scenes (II.i and II.ii) is also indicative of the masterly construction of the play. To see it merely as a revenge tragedy is to miss its complexity – its presentation of a great historical drama, its quality as a major political play and its claim to be the tragedy of Marcus Brutus. Here, for the first time, Shakespeare has created a multifaceted play which is not amenable to categorisation. The most helpful evasion is to describe it as a Roman play. This inability to 'place' *Julius Caesar* is appropriate for a drama which has at its heart the problem of interpretation. As Cicero puts it during his brief appearance in the storm scene:

Indeed, it is a strange-disposed time:
But men may construe things, after their fashion,
Clean from the purpose of the things themselves.
                    (I.iii.33–5)

Throughout the play characters are asking vital (and occasionally trivial) questions without ever gaining unequivocal answers. Brutus agonises over the question of whether it is right to assassinate Caesar (his historical counterpart was most concerned about whether or not the plot would succeed). He has then to decide the fate of Antony, and having done so he has to respond to his request to speak at Caesar's funeral. Later, there is the question of where the battle should take place. Finally, in the event of failure, should he commit suicide – even though, reflecting on Cato's death, he has condemned the act as cowardly. Cassius seems to have no reservations about participating in the assassination but is at variance with Brutus on all the key decisions thereafter – and gives way on every occasion. Even then, all might have been well but for the fact that this man, whose 'sight was ever thick' (v.iii.21), totally misinterprets the fate of Titinius. Titinius' comment is redolent with meaning for the action as a whole: 'Alas, thou hast misconstrued everything' (v.iii.84). Again Cassius experiences a severe weakening of the principles that have guided his life, when, as the final battle draws near, he begins to believe in fate:

You know that I held Epicurus strong,
And his opinion; now I change my mind,
And partly credit things that do presage.
                    (v.i.77–9)

Not only do men misinterpret things, but as they draw near to death they lose faith in the philosophical principles that have guided their lives. The great Caesar himself, Cassius affirms, 'is superstitious grown of late' (II.i.195). Yet, superstitious or not, he fails to detect any message in the terrifying events of the night preceding the Ides of March, being content to adopt a fatalistic attitude and to counter Calphurnia's fears with aphorisms:

Caes.   What can be avoided
            Whose end is purpos'd by the mighty gods?
            Yet Caesar shall go forth; for these predictions
            Are to the world in general as to Caesar.
Cal.   When beggars die, there are no comets seen;
            The heavens themselves blaze forth the death of princes.

Caes. Cowards die many times before their deaths;
The valiant never taste of death but once.
Of all the wonders that I yet have heard,
It seems to me most strange that men should fear,
Seeing that death, a necessary end,
Will come when it will come.

(II.ii.26–37)

When the augurers support Calphurnia, Caesar, instead of acting cautiously, reinterprets the evidence:

Caes.   What say the augurers?
Serv. They would not have you to stir forth to-day.
Plucking the entrails of an offering forth,
They could not find a heart within the beast.
Caes. The gods do this in shame of cowardice:
Caesar should be a beast without a heart
If he should stay at home to-day for fear.

(II.ii.37–43)

Here Caesar seems positively perverse. His behaviour, irrational rather than sceptical, is determined by his self-image.

For all their philosophy and their conception of themselves as 'noble Romans', these self-conscious men are very human. Even when attempting to assume a persona the true personality breaks through, as it does with Casca's denigration of Caesar: he is ostensibly detached, but exhibits the envy and malice of the small man attempting to belittle a great one. Indeed, in the storm scene, when the persona slips, the little man is so small and so changed that some critics have perceived an entirely different character, judging this to be artistic failure by Shakespeare – a rare but significant lapse. The reality of flesh and blood as a counterforce to principles or theory runs right through the play. When Brutus instructs his fellow conspirators to 'carve him as a dish fit for the gods,/Not hew him as a carcass fit for hounds' (II.i.173–4), the image repels by its monstrous distortion of reality. The enactment of the deed leads to horrified recoil by the audience. The perpetrators of the act appear barely rational as their heightened emotional state leads them to make absurd 'philosophical' generalisations before attempting to make a physical reality of Brutus' verbal transformation of murder to sacrifice. Finally, they freeze the historic moment and project themselves into the future. Thus the actors become observers of their own action and by so doing secure detachment and freedom from the bloodiness of the deed:

Cas. Stoop then, and wash. How many ages hence
         Shall this our lofty scene be acted over,
         In states unborn, and accents yet unknown!
Bru. How many times shall Caesar bleed in sport,
         That now on Pompey's basis lies along,
         No worthier than the dust!
Cas.   So oft as that shall be,
         So often shall the knot of us be call'd
         The men that gave their country liberty.
                                        (iii.i.111–18)

It is as if the audience and the conspirators change places: the audience experiences the reality of the slaughter while the conspirators gain the detachment of historical distance. It is a strange and truly fascinating moment – but once more the interpretation is questionable. Cassius' prediction is mistaken on two counts. The deed failed to secure the intended freedom and the verdict of history remains open. Moments later Antony stands over the fallen Caesar and what strikes him most forcibly is blood – 'the most noble blood of all this world' (iii.i.156). Caesar is seen as a victim rather than a sacrifice and the conspirators as hunters and butchers, their noble action as a 'foul deed' that 'shall smell above the earth' (iii.i.274). It is not the spilling of blood that disgusts Antony but the shedding of Caesar's 'costly blood' (iii.i.258) – the price of which will be the shedding of much more blood, including that of innocents. Antony's instinct is to: 'Cry havoc and let slip the dogs of war' (iii.i.273). Caesar's bloody robe, and the corpse itself, will be used by Antony like stage props to incite the crowd and mark Cinna the poet as the first victim in a long line that will stretch to Philippi, encompassing Portia, Brutus, Cassius, Titinius and Marcus Cato, Portia's brother. Ironically, the Brutus who wanted to capture the spirit rather than the body destroys the body and fails signally to destroy the spirit. It first haunts him and then finds reincarnation in the form of Octavius Caesar.

Depite his immensely sympathetic appeal, the treatment of Marcus Brutus is too ironic to bear the full weight of tragic hero. He never gains a clear understanding of his own mistakes and of what went wrong and why. His dying reflection:

                    – Countrymen,
         My heart doth joy that yet in all my life
         I found no man but he was true to me.
                                        (v.v.33–5)

is no doubt true and is truly moving but it is undercut by his seeming failure to realise that in order to fulfil what he saw as his public duty he betrayed Julius Caesar. Their relationship, however, is given sufficient ambiguity to deflect thought of a Judas-like betrayal, but it is sufficiently in evidence to trigger an awareness in the audience of a certain moral blindness in Brutus. Likewise, Brutus reveals no understanding of the political inheritance he bequeaths to Rome; he remains confident that he has acted rightly and that history will vindicate him:

> I shall have glory by this losing day
> More than Octavius and Mark Antony
> By this vile conquest shall attain unto.
>   (v.v.36–8)

The play exhibits a perpetual shifting in the balance of interest and of sympathy between characters – something quite uncharacteristic in Shakespeare's mainstream tragedies – and this continues even in the final phase. Antony regains some of the stature and sympathy previously lost, especially in the proscription scene, by his generous encomium on Brutus; while Octavius exhibits a quiet and persistent astuteness which suggests he is the man of the future. And as interest continues to shift between characters it moves, too, towards a contemplation of history and politics. The concluding phase of the play looks towards the future while consideration of the past provokes an assessment of what has happened and how things might have turned out differently. In particular the play generates that dynamic tension in which events, once they have occurred, carry with them a feeling of inevitability, and yet calls forth analysis in the belief that outcomes are ultimately determined by big decisions, such as Brutus' judgement on Antony, and small things, such as Cassius' misinterpretation of Titinius' fate.

Recently, Paul N. Siegel has expressed the view that: 'Both English and Roman history are shown as guided by providence.'[1] According to this view human beings are prisoners of the past or of a guiding providence which shapes history. They are, therefore, tragic victims of circumstance, with the exception of those who are the agents of providence such as Octavius Caesar. There is no doubt that this perception exists in the minds of the characters and the audience but it is one of a number of competing perceptions. At other times characters feel that they can shape history according to their ideals. They succumb to the vision of a pre-ordained future only when they are losing or lose faith in themselves. Before battles, characters frequently wish that they were able to predict the outcome – a conception which might imply a pre-ordained or pre-determined future. Yet up to that point they do not believe that things are pre-determined and even wanting to know the result in advance does not necessarily signify that they adhere to a belief in a pre-determined outcome. Moreover, Shakespeare makes clear the crucial nature of decisions in influencing events. Brutus makes a series of bad decisions, beginning with his insistence on sparing Antony's life, but even his subsequent blunders, allowing Antony's Forum speech, for example, might not have ended in defeat had he accepted Cassius' advice for the location of the final battle or had there not been a crucial misunderstanding in which Brutus gave the word too early, and later failed to rush to the aid of Cassius. The striking feature of the history plays in general, and *Julius Caesar* in particular, is the sense of *autonomy* they generate. Cassius begins to believe in a pre-ordained destiny only when his judgement tells him that the campaign is being handled badly. It is the processes of disillusionment and enervation which lead people to doubt their capacity to determine events. Far from implying a deterministic view of history, Shakespeare rather shows how everyone gives way to such perceptions at *some time*. However, Ann Molan, who sees the play as 'concerned with the mystery of man's *fate* – especially the fate of Caesar and of Brutus and of Cassius', believes that 'it fails to find a way of probing this to its centre in the flexible dramatic terms necessary to avoid confusing fate with determinism or superstition.'[2]

What several critics do is to provide a conceptual framework which supposedly informed Shakespeare's dramatic representation of historical events. The spontaneity amd vitality of the plays are seen as surface features superimposed on this basic structure. The view articulated here is that Shakespeare was guided not by any such thesis about providence or historical necessity but rather that he explored historical 'moments', vivifying them with characters who are alive and spontaneous, conscious of themselves and of others, breathing the values of their society, motivated by a range of impulses from ambition to the desire to be an ideal Roman, aware of their historical inheritance and aspiring to shape the future in accordance with their ideals. Their sense of destiny is not one of historical inevitability but an awareness of past achievement and future opportunities. These are the makers of history, not actors performing in accordance with a pre-ordained script. They see themselves as water, shaping a course, not as a conduit through which passes the vital current of history. Shakespeare reveals no theology or ideology; he shares with his audience his fascination with characters and events. What he frequently does is to remind us of our tendency to think in terms of historical inevitability when looking backwards, and the tendency people have when facing failure and defeat also to think in these terms.

For all the talk of Julius Caesar's spirit triumphing over the conspirators, his is a pyrrhic victory. He dies at the height of his greatness by surrendering himself to the image of the great man, the infallible leader and father of his people. History suggests that this pattern is so characteristic as to be virtually inevitable, a kind of illness which overtakes dictators. Shakespeare's achievement is momentous partly because he is able to reveal the fineness and greatness of the real man Julius Caesar and the gap which separates the man from the image, with all its poignancy and absurdity. *Julius Caesar* is, then, a profound political study, a fascinating examination of history, an exploration of a specific culture and an intriguing psychological analysis of men, both as men and as political beings. In adopting this multifaceted approach Shakespeare shows a remarkably disciplined control of language. All the devices of rhetoric are fully exploited yet there is never a sense of verbal extravagance: the medium of language is made to serve the dramatic design to such an extent that it has been perceived, mistakenly, as sparse. The language has been adapted totally to the culture of Rome and to the characters who inhabit it. Yet, it possesses a texture that is both rich and colourful. Antony reveals a perfect understanding of the common man *en masse*. His Forum speech, with its enormous range of suggestion and delicacy of nuance, is the greatest example of the persuasive power of oratory in the whole of Shakespeare. At the other extreme is the quarrel between Brutus and Cassius with its emotional swings and collisions between public postures – 'For I am arm'd so strong in honesty' (IV.iii.67) – to the intimately childlike 'You love me not' (IV.iii.88). Again there is the contrast between Casca's maliciously witty description of the crown-offering and Portia's passionate plea to the man she loves. Metaphors, which so often in Shakespeare seem to spawn whole generations of offspring, are generally taut and restrained. When resorted to, as in Brutus' orchard soliloquy, they are untrustworthy. It is as if in this culture thought finds expression in a controlled and modulated way. Only Brutus and Julius Caesar make significant resort to metaphors and then generally under the strain of emotional pressure. This is not to suggest an absence of imagery, as there are a great many images of metal, body parts, animals and birds, blood, etc. Moreover, the conceptual imagery relating to hands, hearts, love and acting is potent. All the resources of language are put to use, but the striking stylistic feature of this play is the control which generates a feeling of linguistic tautness, reflecting perfectly the nature of the social universe and the tensions generated by the competing pulls of human spontaneity and commitment to a public life.

It is not necessary to be a Marxist or a new historicist to appreciate that when first performed the impact of this play was potentially explosive. Here authority, and the contention for political power, are thoroughly inter-rogated, quite free from any counterpart of the 'divinity' that 'doth hedge a king'. Moreover, as Drakakis and others have pointed out, here is an intriguing reflexivity which underlines the political nature of theatre – and the theatrical nature of politics. Here is Rome – but also Elizabethan England; here are theatrical props possessing both the persuasive potency and illusory qualities of ideological constructs. The play raises questions about historical events to which it refuses to provide answers. Likewise, it raises vital questions about ideology, power and conflict, and sends the audience out of the theatre provoked into wondering about the precise nature of the social and political world they inhabit – and its susceptibility to change. The juices of the play continue to flow because the issues are still alive.

Notes

PREFACE

1. The German text was first published by Gustav Binz, *Anglia*, 22 (1899), p. 456, and is reprinted in E. K. Chambers, *The Elizabethan Stage*, 4 vols. (Clarendon Press: Oxford, 1923), vol. 2, p. 364, with an English translation, p. 365. The translation provided here is from T. S. Dorsch (ed.), *Julius Caesar* (The Arden Shakespeare, Methuen: London and New York, 1972; first published 1955), p. vii.
2. See Martin Spevack (ed.), *Julius Caesar* (The New Cambridge Shakespeare, Cambridge University Press: Cambridge, 1988), p. 6.
3. Helen Gardner, *Religion and Literature* (Faber & Faber: London, 1971), p. 69.
4. M. C. Bradbrook, *Shakespeare the Craftsman: The Clark Lectures* (Chatto & Windus: London, 1969), p. 97.
5. Anne Barton, '*Julius Caesar* and *Coriolanus*: Shakespeare's Roman world of words', in Philip H. Highfill (ed.), *Shakespeare's Craft* (Southern Illinois University Press: Carbondale, Ill., 1982), pp. 25 and 43.
6. Laurence Lerner (ed.), *Reconstructing Literature* (Blackwell: Oxford, 1983), p. 3.

111

7. George Steiner, *The Sunday Times*, 4 May 1980, p. 43, cited by Lerner, p. 4.

8. Cedric Watts, 'Bottom's children', in Lerner, pp. 20–35.

9. Jonathan Dollimore and Alan Sinfield (eds.), *Political Shakespeare: New essays in cultural materialism* (Manchester University Press: Manchester, 1985), pp. viii, 10 and 131–2.

10. Jean E. Howard and Marion F. O'Connor (eds.), *Shakespeare Reproduced: The text in history and ideology* (Methuen: New York and London, 1987), p. 4.

11. Walter Cohen, 'Political criticism of Shakespeare', in *ibid.*, p. 35.

12. James H. Kavanagh, 'Shakespeare in Ideology', in John Drakakis (ed.), *Alternative Shakespeares* (Methuen: London and New York, 1985), pp. 149 and 151.

13. L. C. Knights, *Drama and Society in the Age of Jonson* (Peregrine Books: London, 1962; first published by Chatto & Windus, 1937), pp. 41–2.

14. J. W. Lever, *The Tragedy of State* (Methuen: London, 1971), pp. 2–5.

15. Cohen, pp. 33–4 and 26.

16. Anne Barton, 'Perils of historicism', review of Stephen Greenblatt's *Learning to Curse: Essays in early modern culture*, *New York Review of Books*, 28 March 1991, pp. 51 and 54.

17. Richard Levin, 'Unthinkable thoughts in the new historicizing of English Renaissance drama', *New Literary History*, no. 5 (Spring 1990), pp. 434–43.

18. Watts, p. 35.

19. John Drakakis, '"Fashion it thus": *Julius Caesar* and the politics of theatrical representation', paper delivered to the 24th International Shakespeare Conference at the Shakespeare Institute, Stratford-upon-Avon, August 1990, published in *ShS*, 44 (1992), pp. 67 and 72.

THE STAGE HISTORY

1. Arthur Humphries (ed.), *Julius Caesar*, (Oxford Shakespeare, Oxford University Press: Oxford, 1984), p. 52.

2. John Ripley, *'Julius Caesar' on Stage in England and America 1599–1973* (Cambridge University Press: Cambridge, 1980), p. 50.

3. Humphries, pp. 54–5.

4. *Ibid.*, p. 57.

5. W. C. Macready, *Reminiscences*, ed. F. Pollock, 2 vols. (1875), cited by Humphries, p. 57.

6. Ripley, pp. 88–9.

7. *Ibid.*, p. 99.
8. George C. D. Odell, *Shakespeare from Betterton to Irving*, 2 vols. (Dover Publications: New York, 1966; first published by Charles Scribner's Sons: New York, 1920), vol. 2, pp. 450–1; see his comments on the Saxe-Meiningen Company, pp. 423–5.
9. Cited by Ripley, p. 154.
10. Muriel St Clare Byrne, 'Fifty years of Shakespearian production', *ShS*, 2 (1949), cited by Humphries, p. 64.
11. Ripley, pp. 226–30.
12. *Ibid.*, pp. 196, 197 and 199.
13. *Ibid.*, p. 235.
14. *Ibid.*, p. 237, includes a quotation from *The Times*, 21 January 1930.
15. *Ibid.*, pp. 239–40.
16. *Ibid.*, pp. 243–4.
17. *Ibid.*, pp. 247–9.
18. *Ibid.*, pp. 252–3.
19. *Ibid.*, p. 256.
20. Roy Walker, 'Unto Caesar: a review of recent productions', *ShS*, 11 (1958), p. 132, cited by Ripley, p. 256.
21. Ripley, pp. 257–8.
22. *Ibid.*, pp. 266–7.
23. *Ibid.*, pp. 271, 274, 272, 273–4.
24. *Ibid.*, p. 275.
25. Douglas Campbell, Director's Preface to the Festival Edition of *Julius Caesar*, p. 265, edited by John Saxton, Toronto, 1970, p. xxxiii, cited by Ripley, p. 265.

THE CRITICAL RECEPTION

1. Ernest Schanzer, *The Problem Plays of Shakespeare: A study of 'Julius Caesar', 'Measure for Measure' and 'Antony and Cleopatra'* (Routledge: London, 1963), p. 10.
2. J. P. Brockbank, 'Myth and history in Shakespeare's Rome', in *On Shakespeare: Jesus, Shakespeare and Karl Marx, and other essays* (Blackwell: Oxford, 1989), p. 143.
3. W. Warde Fowler, *Roman Essays and Interpretations* (Clarendon Press: Oxford, 1911).
4. Willard Farnham, *Shakespeare's Tragic Frontier* (University of California Press: Berkeley, Calif., and Los Angeles, 1950; reprinted 1963).

5. Virgil K. Whitaker, *Shakespeare's Use of Learning* (Huntington Library: San Marino, Calif., 1953).

6. Harley Granville-Barker, *Prefaces to Shakespeare: 'Julius Caesar' and 'Antony and Cleopatra'* (Batsford: London, 1984; first published 1930), pp. 8–9.

7. C. H. Herford, *Ben Jonson*, 2 vols. (Clarendon Press: Oxford, 1925), in Peter Ure (ed.), *Shakespeare's 'Julius Caesar'* (Casebook Series, Macmillan, London, 1969), pp. 49–50.

8. G. Wilson Knight, *The Imperial Theme: Further interpretations of Shakespeare's tragedies including the Roman plays* (Third edition first published by Methuen University Paperback: London, 1965; first edition published by Oxford University Press: Oxford, 1931), p. 63.

CHAPTER 1

1. Dorsch, p. xxiii.

2. Humphries, p. 73.

3. Fredson Bowers, 'The copy for Shakespeare's *Julius Caesar*', *SAB*, 43 (1978), pp. 23–36, cited by Humphries, p. 73.

4. John Dover Wilson (ed.), *Julius Caesar* (The New Cambridge Shakespeare, Cambridge University Press: Cambridge, 1949), pp. 96–7.

5. Granville-Barker, p. 33.

6. Norman Sanders (ed.), *Julius Caesar* (New Penguin Shakespeare, Penguin: Harmondsworth, 1967), p. 11. See also Spevack, p. 11.

7. Wilson, p. 96.

8. Ben Jonson, *Timber: or Discoveries; Made upon Men and Matter*, in Ure ed., (Macmillan Casebook), pp. 27–8.

9. John Palmer, *Political and Comic Characters of Shakespeare* (Macmillan: London, 1962), pp. 44–5.

10. John Dover Wilson, 'Ben Jonson and *Julius Caesar*', *ShS*, 2 (1949), p. 41.

11. Humphries, pp. 79–81.

12. Granville-Barker, pp. 67–9.

13. Humphries, pp. 80–1.

14. Alexander Leggatt, *Shakespeare's Political Drama: The history plays and the Roman plays* (Routledge: London and New York, 1988), p. 148.

15. Palmer, p. 56.

16. Brents Stirling, 'Brutus and the death of Portia', *SQ*, 10 (1959), pp. 211–17.

17. A. D. Nuttall, *A New Mimesis: Shakespeare and the representation of reality* (Methuen: London and New York, 1983), p. 112.

18. K. Muir, *Shakespeare's Tragic Sequence* (Hutchinson University Library: London, 1972), p. 51.

19. Thomas Healy, *New Latitudes: Theory and English Renaissance Literature* (Edward Arnold: London, 1992), pp. 46–7.

20. Ann Thompson, 'Does it matter which edition you use?' in Lesley Aers and Nigel Wheale (eds), *Shakespeare in the Changing Curriculum* (Routledge: London and New York, 1991), p. 84.

21. Norman Sanders, p. 24.

22. See for instance T. McAlindon's interesting formulation of this issue in *Shakespeare's Tragic Cosmos* (Cambridge University Press: Cambridge, 1991), p. 94.

CHAPTER 2

1. For commentary on this issue see K. Muir, *The Singularity of Shakespeare and Other Essays* (Liverpool University Press: Liverpool, 1977), p. 2, and J. Wilders, *The Lost Garden: A view of Shakespeare's English and Roman history plays* (Macmillan: London and Basingstoke, 1978), pp. 3–4.

2. Wilders, pp. 1, 5–6.

3. Muir, *The Singularity of Shakespeare*, p. 1.

4. Jonathan Dollimore, *Radical Tragedy: Religion, ideology and power in the drama of Shakespeare and his contemporaries* (Harvester: Brighton, 1984), pp. 189–202; R. S. White, '*King Lear* and philosophical anarchism', *English*, vol. xxxvii, no. 159 (Autumn 1988), pp. 181–200.

5. Spevack, p. 30.

6. Clifford Leech, 'Shakespeare's tragic fiction', *Annual Lecture of the British Academy*, LIX (1973), p. 8.

7. Irving Ribner, *Patterns in Shakespearian Tragedy* (Methuen/Barnes & Noble: London, 1960; latest reprint, 1971), p. 37.

8. Reuben Brower, *Hero and Saint: Shakespeare and the Graeco-Roman heroic tradition* (Clarendon Press: Oxford, 1971), p. 226.

9. Humphries, p. 34.

10. John Bayley, *Shakespeare and Tragedy* (Routledge & Kegan Paul: London, 1981), p. 124.

11. Humphries, pp. 32–3.

12. Robert S. Miola, *Shakespeare's Rome* (Cambridge University Press: New York and Cambridge, 1983), p. 17.

13. John W. Velz, 'The ancient world in Shakespeare: authenticity or anachronism? A retrospect', *ShS*, 31 (1978), pp. 11–12.

14. Charles and Michelle Martindale, *Shakespeare and the Uses of Antiquity* (Routledge: London, 1990), pp. 126–7, 122.
15. Cicero, *De Officiis*, Walter Miller trans. (The Loeb Classical Library; Harvard University Press: Cambridge, Mass., 1913), pp. 292–3.
16. William B. Toole, 'The cobbler, the disrobed image and the motif of movement in *Julius Caesar*', *The Upstart Crow*, vol. iv, (Fall 1982), pp. 41–55.
17. W. Warde Fowler, *Roman Essays and Interpretations*, in Ure, p. 49.
18. Farnham, pp. 3–4.
19. H. B. Charlton, *Shakespeare, Politics and Politicians*, The English Association Pamphlet no. 72 (April 1929), pp. 23 and 19. See also Charlton's *Shakespearian Tragedy* (Cambridge University Press: Cambridge, 1948), especially Introduction and pp. 69–82.
20. Wilson (ed.), *Julius Caesar*, p. xx.
21. Schanzer, pp. 68 and 70.
22. Norman Rabkin, 'Structure, convention and meaning in *Julius Caesar*', *JEGP*, lxiii (1964), in Ure, pp. 104–5.
23. Nicholas Brooke, *Shakespeare's Early Tragedies* (Methuen: London, 1968), p. 162.
24. James C. Bulman, *The Heroic Idiom of Shakespearian Tragedy* (University of Delaware Press: Newark; and Associated University Presses: London and Toronto, 1985), pp. 56–60.
25. W. Nicholas Knight, 'Brutus' motivation and melancholy', *The Upstart Crow*, vol. v (Fall 1984), p. 122.
26. Alan Hager, '"The teeth of emulation": failed sacrifice in Shakespeare's *Julius Caesar*', *The Upstart Crow*, vol. viii (1988), p. 64.
27. Robert S. Miola, 'Shakespeare and his sources: observations on the critical history of *Julius Caesar*', *Shakespeare Survey*, 40 (1988), p. 73.
28. Humphries, p. 16.
29. L. C. Knights, *Further Explorations* (Chatto & Windus: London; and Stanford University Press: Stanford, Calif., 1965), p. 34.
30. Brents Stirling, *Unity in Shakespearian Tragedy: The interplay of theme and character* (Columbia University Press, New York, 1956), in Alfred Harbage (ed.), *Shakespeare: The Tragedies: A collection of critical essays* (Twentieth Century Views, Prentice Hall: Englewood Cliffs, New Jersey, 1964), pp. 37, 41–2.
31. Geoffrey Bullough (ed.), *Narrative and Dramatic Sources of Shakespeare: Vol. v. The Roman plays* (Routledge: London, 1964), p. 52.
32. Granville-Barker, p. 60.
33. Leggatt, p. 158.
34. Paul N. Siegel, *Shakespeare's English and Roman History Plays: A*

Marxist approach (Associated University Presses: New Jersey, London and Toronto, 1986), p. 108.
35. Charles and Michelle Martindale, p. 142.
36. Palmer, p. x.

CHAPTER 3

1. James R. Siemon, *Shakespearean Iconoclasm* (University of California Press: Berkeley, Calif., 1985), pp. 115–19.
2. Bullough, p. 103.
3. *Ibid.*, p. 66.
4. *Ibid.*, pp. 78–86.
5. *Ibid.*, pp. 17–18.
6. Suetonius, *The History of Twelve Caesars* (1606), Philemon Holland trans., in Bullough, p. 149.
7. Schanzer (ed.), *Shakespeare's Appian: Selected reprints from the 1578 translation of Bella Civilia* (Liverpool University Press: Liverpool, 1956), pp. 66 and 8, cited by Schanzer, *The Problem Plays of Shakespeare*, p. 15. All subsequent Schanzer references are to this source.
8. Schanzer, pp. 11 and 16.
9. Maurice Charney, *Shakespeare's Roman Plays: The function of imagery in the drama* (Harvard University Press: Cambridge, Mass., 1961), p. 67, and for a very similar statement see G. Wilson Knight, p. 65.
10. Mark Hunter, 'Politics and characters in Shakespeare's *Julius Caesar*', from Royal Society of Literature, *Essays by Diverse Hands*, x (1931); also in Ure (ed.), p. 196.
11. Palmer, pp. 35–6.
12. Granville-Barker, p. 34.
13. G. Wilson Knight, p. 72.
14. Edward Dowden, *Shakespeare: A critical study of his mind and art* (Routledge & Kegan Paul: London, 1875), p. 285.
15. Plutarch's *Lives* in Bullough, pp. 88–110.
16. *Ibid.*, pp. 119–24.
17. *Ibid.*, pp. 127–35.
18. Norman Sanders, p. 19.
19. Dowden, p. 283.
20. Hunter, in Ure, p. 204.
21. G. Wilson Knight, pp. 78 and 80–1.
22. Hugh M. Richmond, *Shakespeare's Political Plays* (Random House: New York, 1967), cited by Leonard F. Dean (ed.), *Twentieth Century*

Interpretations of 'Julius Caesar': A collection of critical essays (Prentice Hall: Englewood Cliffs, New Jersey, 1968), pp. 103–4.
23. Knights, *Further Explorations*, p. 51.
24. William and Barbara Rosen, 'Julius Caesar: "The speciality of rule"', in Dean, p. 112.
25. G. Wilson Knight, *The Wheel of Fire: Interpretations of Shakespearian tragedy* (Methuen: London, 1949, 4th edn; first published by Oxford University Press: Oxford, 1930), p. 124.
26. Schanzer, pp. 55–6.
27. Granville-Barker, p. 11.
28. Rabkin, in Ure, p. 107.
29. Siemon, p. 16.
30. William O. Scott, 'The speculative eye: problematic self-knowledge in *Julius Caesar*', *ShS*, 40 (1988), p. 83.
31. Leggatt, p. 144.
32. Samuel Taylor Coleridge, *Shakespearian Criticism, Vol. 1*, ed. Thomas Middleton, 2 vols. (J. M. Dent: London, 1960), p. 14.
33. Nuttall, pp. 107–9.
34. Wilders, pp. 133–4.
35. Schanzer, p. 49.
36. Palmer, pp. 22–3.
37. Granville-Barker, p. 49.
38. Schanzer, p. 65.
39. Palmer, pp. 54–5.
40. Siemon, pp. 174–5.
41. Leggatt, pp. 150–1.
42. Granville-Barker, pp. 56–7.
43. G. Wilson Knight, *The Imperial Theme*, pp. 82 and 74–5.
44. Leggatt, p. 150.
45. Julian C. Rice, 'Julius Caesar and the judgement of the senses', *SEL*, 13 (1973), pp. 239–43, 254; Moody E. Prior, 'The search for a hero in *Julius Caesar*', *RenD* (n.s.) 2 (1969), pp. 90–3; Norman Rabkin, *Shakespeare and the Common Understanding* (Free Press: New York, 1967), pp. 117–18; Mildred Hartsock, 'The complexity of *Julius Caesar*', *PMLA*, 81 (1966), pp. 60–2.
46. Ralph Rader, 'Fact, theory, and literary explanation', *Critical Inquiry*, 1 (1974), p. 253.
47. Richard Levin, 'Shakespearean defects and Shakespeareans' Defences', in Maurice Charney (ed.), *'Bad' Shakespeare: Revaluations of the Shakespeare canon* (Associated University Presses: London, New York, Ontario, 1988), p. 30.

48. Plutarch's *Lives* in Bullough, pp. 257, 269, 320, 140, 319.
49. Appian, *The Civil Wars*, in Bullough, pp. 157–9.
50. David Daiches, 'Guilt and justice in Shakespeare: *Julius Caesar*', in *Literary Essays* (University of Chicago Press: Chicago, Ill., 1956), in Dean, p. 71.
51. Granville-Barker, pp. 22–3.
52. *Ibid.*, p. 28.
53. Ann Molan, '*Julius Caesar*: The general good and the singular case' *CR*, 26 (1984), p. 93.
54. William Hazlitt, *Characters of Shakespeare's Plays*, ed. Ernest Rhys (Everyman Library, J. M. Dent: London, Toronto, New York, 1906), p. 29.
55. Dowden, p. 294.
56. Molan, p. 91.

CHAPTER 4

1. Velz, p. 9.
2. Mark Van Doren, *Shakespeare* (Doubleday, New York, 1953: first published by Holt, Rinehart and Winston Inc.: London and New York, 1939), pp. 155, 153.
3. Bradbrook, p. 103.
4. Humphries, pp. 42, 46–8.
5. Charles and Michelle Martindale, p. 139.
6. G. Wilson Knight, *The Imperial Theme*, pp. 63, 44.
7. Bradbrook, p. 107.
8. Siemon, p. 126.
9. Alessandro Serpieri, 'Reading the signs: towards a semiotics of Shakespearean drama', in Drakakis (ed.), *Alternative Shakespeares*, pp. 132–4.
10. Brooke, p. 150.
11. Norman Sanders, 'The shift of power in *Julius Caesar*', *REL*, vol. v, no. 2 (April 1964), p. 27.
12. Geoffrey Bullough, 'The uses of history', in J. Sutherland and J. Hurstfield (eds.), *Shakespeare's World* (Edward Arnold: London, 1964), p. 112.
13. Bulman, p. 60.
14. Hager, p. 54.
15. Charney, *Shakespeare's Roman Plays*, pp. 1–78.
16. Gunter Walch, ' "Caesar did never wrong, but with just cause":

Interrogative dramatic structure in *Julius Caesar*'. Paper delivered at the 24th International Shakespeare Conference, Shakespeare Institute, Stratford-upon-Avon, August 1990.

17. Drakakis, 'Fashion it thus', *ShS*, 44 (1992), pp. 69 and 71.
18. Barbara J. Baines, 'Political and poetic revisionism in *Julius Caesar*', *The Upstart Crow*, vol. x (1990), pp. 42 and 52.
19. Healy, pp. 43–5.
20. R. A. Foakes, 'An approach to *Julius Caesar*', *SQ*, 5 (1954), pp. 259–70, reprinted in Dean, pp. 60–3.
21. Hager, pp. 59–60.
22. Baines, p. 51.

CHAPTER 5

1. Siegel, p. 135.
2. Molan, p. 84.

Select Bibliography

The following abbreviations are used throughout for journal entries:

AI	American Imago
BSUF	Ball State University Forum
BuR	Bucknell Review
CahiersE	Cahiers Elisabéthains
CentR	Centennial Review (Mich. State U.)
CLAJ	College Language Association Journal (Morgan State Coll., Baltimore)
CompD	Comparative Drama
	Costerus: Essays in English and American Language and Literature (Amsterdam)
CR	Critical Review (Melbourne; Sydney)
CritQ	Critical Quarterly
EJ	English Journal
ELH	Journal of English Literary History
ELR	English Literary Renaissance
ES	English Studies. A Journal of English Letters and Philology (Amsterdam)
HLQ	Huntington Library Quarterly

JEGP	Journal of English and Germanic Philology
JHI	Journal of the History of Ideas
L&P	Literature and Psychology (U. of Hartford and Fairleigh Dickinson U.)
LC	Library Chronicle (U. of Pennsylvania)
MLR	Modern Language Review
NLH	New Literary History (U. of Virginia)
PMLA	Publications of the Modern Language Association of America
PsyR	Psychoanalytic Review
REL	Review of English Literature (London)
RenD	Renaissance Drama
RenQ	Renaissance Quarterly
RES	Review of English Studies
SAB	South Atlantic Bulletin
SEL	Studies in English Literature, 1500–1900
ShakS	Shakespeare Studies (U. of Cincinnati and others)
ShS	Shakespeare Survey
SoR	Southern Review (Louisiana State U.)
SP	Studies in Philology
SQ	Shakespeare Quarterly
SR	Sewanee Review
	Theoria: A Journal of Studies in the Arts, Humanities and Social Sciences (Natal)
TSLL	Texas Studies in Literature and Language [Supersedes UTSE]
UR	University Review [Supersedes UKCR]
YR	Yale Review

Books

Bayley, J., *Shakespeare and Tragedy* (Routledge & Kegan Paul: London, 1981).

Bonjour, A., *The Structure of 'Julius Caesar'* (University of Liverpool Press: Liverpool, 1958).

Bradbrook, M. C., *Shakespeare the Craftsman: The Clark Lectures* (Chatto & Windus: London, 1969).

Brockbank, J. P., *On Shakespeare: Jesus, Shakespeare and Karl Marx, and other essays* (Blackwell: Oxford, 1989).

Brooke, Nicholas, *Shakespeare's Early Tragedies* (Methuen: London, 1968).

Brower, R. A., *Hero and Saint: Shakespeare and the Graeco-Roman heroic tradition* (Clarendon Press: Oxford, 1971).

Brown, John Russell, *Shakespeare's Dramatic Style* (Heinemann: London, 1970).

Bullough, G. (ed.), *Narrative and Dramatic Sources of Shakespeare: Vol. v. The Roman plays* (Routledge: London, 1964).

Bulman, J. C., *The Heroic Idiom of Shakespearian Tragedy* (University of Delaware Press: Newark; Associated University Presses: London and Toronto, 1985).

Burke, K., *Language as Symbolic Action* (University of California Press: Berkeley, Calif., 1966).

Cantor, Paul A., *Shakespeare's Rome: Republic and empire* (Cornell University Press: Ithaca, New York, and London, 1976).

Champion, L. S., *Shakespeare's Tragic Perspective: The development of his tragic technique* (University of Georgia Press: Athens, Ga., 1976).

Charlton, H. B., *Shakespeare, Politics and Politicians*, The English Association Pamphlet no. 72 (April 1929).

Charlton, H. B., *Shakespearian Tragedy* (Cambridge University Press: Cambridge, 1948).

Charney, Maurice, *Shakespeare's Roman Plays: The function of imagery in the drama* (Harvard University Press: Cambridge, Mass., 1961).

Charney, Maurice (ed.), *Discussions of Shakespeare's Roman Plays* (D. C. Heath: Boston, Mass., 1964).

Charney, Maurice (ed.), *'Bad' Shakespeare: Revaluations of the Shakespeare canon* (Associated University Presses: London, New York, Ontario, 1988).

Clarke, M. L., *The Noblest Roman: Marcus Brutus and his reputation* (Thames & Hudson: London, 1981).

Colie, R., *The Resources of Kind: Genre theory in the Renaissance* (University of California Press: Berkeley, Calif., and Los Angeles, 1973).

Cox, C. B. and D. J. Palmer (eds.), *Shakespeare's Wide and Universal Stage* (Manchester University Press: Manchester, 1984).

Daiches, David, *Shakespeare: 'Julius Caesar'*, Studies in English Literature no. 65 (Edward Arnold: London, 1976).

Danson, L., *Tragic Alphabet: Shakespeare's drama of language* (Yale University Press: New Haven, Conn., and London, 1974).

Dean, Leonard F. (ed.), *Twentieth Century Interpretations of 'Julius Caesar': A collection of critical essays* (Prentice Hall: Englewood Cliffs, New Jersey, 1968).

Dessen, A. C., *Elizabethan Drama and the Viewer's Eye* (University of North Carolina Press: Chapel Hill, North Carolina, 1977).

Dowden, Edward, *Shakespeare: A critical study of his mind and art* (Routledge & Kegan Paul: London, 1875).

Draper, R. P., *Tragedy: Developments in criticism* (Macmillan Casebook Series, Macmillan: London, 1980).

Edwards, P., I.-S. Ewbank and G. K. Hunter (eds), *Shakespeare's styles: Essays in honour of Kenneth Muir* (Cambridge University Press: Cambridge, 1980).

Erskine-Hill, H., *The Idea of Augustus in English Literature* (Edward Arnold: London, 1983).

Evans, B., *Shakespeare's Tragic Practice* (Clarendon Press: Oxford, 1979).

Farnham, Willard, *Shakespeare's Tragic Frontier* (University of California Press: Berkeley, Los Angeles, Calif., 1950; reprinted 1963).

Farnham, Willard, *The Medieval Heritage of Elizabethan Tragedy* (Basil Blackwell: Oxford, 1936: reprinted 1970).

Fowler, W. W., *Roman Essays and Interpretations* (Clarendon Press: Oxford, 1911).

Frye, Northrop, *Fools of Time: Studies in Shakespearian tragedy* (University of Toronto Press: Toronto, 1967).

Gardner, Helen, *Religion and Literature* (Faber & Faber: London, 1971).

Granville-Barker, H., *Prefaces to Shakespeare: 'Julius Caesar' and 'Antony and Cleopatra'* (Batsford: London, 1984; first published 1930).

Gundolf, F., *The Mantle of Caesar*, J. W. Hartmann trans. (Macy-Masius, Vanguard: New York, 1928; Cayme: London, 1929).

Harbage, Alfred (ed.), *Shakespeare: The Tragedies: A collection of critical essays* (Twentieth Century Views, Prentice Hall: Englewood Cliffs, New Jersey, 1964).

Hazlitt, William, *Characters of Shakespeare's Plays*, ed., Ernest Rhys (Everyman Library, J. M. Dent: London, Toronto, New York, 1906).

Homan, S., *Shakespeare's Theatre of Presence: Language, spectacle and the audience* (Associated University Presses: London and Toronto, 1986).

Honigmann, E. A. J., *Shakespeare: Seven Tragedies: The dramatist's manipulation of response* (Macmillan, London, 1976).

Honigmann, E. A. J. (ed.), *Shakespeare and his Contemporaries: Essays in comparison* (Revels Plays Companion Library, Manchester University Press: Manchester, 1986).

Houston, J. P., *Shakespearean Sentences: A study in style and syntax* (Louisiana State University Press: Baton Rouge, La., and London, 1988).

Huzar, E. G., *Mark Antony* (Croom Helm/Routledge: London, 1986).

Johnson, S., *Samuel Johnson on Shakespeare*, ed. H. R. Woudhuysen (New Penguin Shakespeare Library, Penguin: London, 1989).

Jones, Emrys, *Scenic Form in Shakespeare* (Clarendon Press: Oxford, 1971).

Jorgensen, Paul A., *William Shakespeare: The tragedies* (University of California Press/Twayne Publishers: Los Angeles, Boston, Mass., 1985).

Kastan, D. S., *Shakespeare and the Shapes of Time* (University Press of New England: Hanover, New Hampshire, 1982).

Knight, G. Wilson, *The Imperial Theme: Further interpretations of Shakespeare's tragedies including the Roman plays* (Methuen: London, 1951, 3rd edn; first published by Oxford University Press, 1931).

Knight, G. Wilson, *The Wheel of Fire: Interpretations of Shakespearian tragedy* (Methuen: London, 1949, 4th edn; first published by Oxford University Press: Oxford, 1930).

Knight, G. Wilson, *Shakespearian Dimensions* (Harvester Press: Brighton; Barnes & Noble: Totowa, New Jersey, 1984).

Knights, L. C., *Drama and Society in the Age of Jonson* (Peregrine Books: London, 1962; first published by Chatto & Windus: London, 1937).

Knights, L. C., *Some Shakespearian Themes* (Chatto & Windus: London, 1959).

Knights, L. C., *Further Explorations* (Chatto & Windus: London; Stanford University Press: Stanford, Calif., 1965).

Kott, Jan, *Shakespeare Our Contemporary* (Methuen: London, 2nd edn rev. 1967).

Leach, J., *Pompey the Great* (Croom Helm/Routledge: London, 1986).

Leech, C., 'Shakespeare's Tragic Fiction', *Annual Lecture of the British Academy*, LIX (1973).

Leggatt, Alexander, *Shakespeare's Political Drama: The history plays and the Roman plays* (Routledge: London and New York, 1988).

Lever, J. W., *The Tragedy of State* (Methuen: London, 1971).

Long, M., *The Unnatural Scene: A study in Shakespearean tragedy* (Methuen: London, 1976).

McAlindon, T., *Shakespeare's Tragic Cosmos* (Cambridge University Press: Cambridge, 1991).

MacCallum, M. W., *Shakespeare's Roman Plays and Their Background* (Macmillan: London, 1910; new edn with introduction by T. J. B. Spencer, 1967).

Mahood, M. M., *Shakespeare's Wordplay* (Methuen: London and New York, 1957).

Markels, Julien (ed.), *Shakespeare's 'Julius Caesar'* (Charles Scribner's Sons: New York, 1961).

Martindale, Charles and Michelle, *Shakespeare and the Uses of Antiquity* (Routledge: London, 1990).

Mehl, Dieter, *Shakespeare's Tragedies: An introduction* (Cambridge University Press: Cambridge, 1986).

Miola, Robert S., *Shakespeare's Rome* (Cambridge University Press: New York and Cambridge, 1983).

Muir, Kenneth, *Shakespeare's Tragic Sequence* (Hutchinson University Library: London, 1972).

Muir, Kenneth, *The Singularity of Shakespeare and Other Essays* (Liverpool University Press: Liverpool, 1977).

Nevo, Ruth, *Tragic Form in Shakespeare* (Princeton University Press: Princeton, New Jersey, 1972).

Nuttall, A. D., *A New Mimesis: Shakespeare and the representation of reality* (Methuen: London and New York, 1983).

Odell, G. C. D., *Shakespeare from Betterton to Irving*, 2 vols. (Dover Publications, New York, 1966; first published by Charles Scribner's Sons, New York, 1920).

Orgel, S., *The Illusion of Power: Political theatre in the English Renaissance* (University of California Press: Berkeley, Calif., 1975).

Osborne, J., *The Meiningen Court Theatre* (Cambridge University Press: Cambridge, New York, New Rochelle, Melbourne, Sydney, 1988).

Palmer, J., *Political and Comic Characters of Shakespeare* (Macmillan: London, 1962).

Payne, M., *Irony in Shakespeare's Roman Plays* (Institut für Englische Sprache und Literatur, 1974).

Phillips, J. E., *The State in Shakespeare's Greek and Roman Plays* (Columbia University Press: New York, 1940).

Platt, M., *Rome and Romans According to Shakespeare* (Universität Salzburg: Salzburg, 1976).

Proser, M. N., *The Heroic Image in Five Shakespearian Tragedies* (Princeton University Press: Princeton, New Jersey, 1965).

Rabkin, Norman, *Shakespeare and the Common Understanding* (Free Press: New York, 1967).

Rabkin, Norman, *Shakespeare and the Problem of Meaning* (University of Chicago Press: Chicago, Ill., 1981).

Ribner, Irving, *Patterns in Shakespearian Tragedy* (Methuen/Barnes & Noble: London, 1960; latest reprint 1971).

Richmond, Hugh M., *Shakespeare's Political Plays* (Random House: New York, 1967).

Ripley, J., *'Julius Caesar' on Stage in England and America 1599–1973* (Cambridge University Press: Cambridge, 1980).

Rosen, William, *Shakespeare and the Craft of Tragedy* (Harvard University Press: Cambridge, Mass., 1960).

Sanders, Wilbur, *The Dramatist and the Received Idea: Studies in the plays of Marlowe and Shakespeare* (Cambridge University Press: Cambridge, 1968).

Schanzer, E., *The Problem Plays of Shakespeare: A study of 'Julius Caesar', 'Measure for Measure' and 'Antony and Cleopatra'* (Routledge: London, 1963).

Siegel, Paul N., *Shakespeare's English and Roman History Plays: A Marxist approach* (Associated University Presses: London and Toronto, 1986).

Siemon, James R., *Shakespearean Iconoclasm* (University of California Press: Berkeley, Calif., 1985).

Simmons, J. L., *Shakespeare's Pagan World: The Roman Tragedies* (University Press of Virginia: Charlottesville, Va., 1973).

Spencer, T. J. B., *Shakespeare: The Roman Plays* (Writers and their Works no. 157, Longman: London, 1963; 2nd edn 1973).

Stapfer, Paul, *Shakespeare and Classical Antiquity: Greek and Latin antiquity as presented in Shakespeare's plays* (a partial translation by Emily J. Carey of *Shakespeare et L'Antiquité*, C. Kegan Paul and Co., London, 1880).

Stirling, Brents, *The Populace in Shakespeare* (Columbia University Press: New York, 1949).

Stirling, Brents, *Unity in Shakespearian Tragedy: The interplay of theme and character* (Columbia University Press: New York, 1956).

Sutherland, J. and J. Hurstfield (eds.), *Shakespeare's World* (Edward Arnold: London, 1964).

Thomas, Vivian, *Shakespeare's Roman Worlds* (Routledge: London, 1989).

Thomson, J. A. K., *Shakespeare and the Classics* (Allen & Unwin: London, 1952).

Traversi, D. A., *Shakespeare: The Roman plays* (Hollis & Carter: London, 1963).

Ure, Peter (ed.), *Shakespeare's 'Julius Caesar'* (Casebook Series, Macmillan, London, 1969).

Van Doren, Mark, *Shakespeare* (Doubleday, New York 1953; first published by Holt, Rinehart & Winston Inc.: London and New York, 1939).

Van Laan, Thomas, F., *Role-Playing in Shakespeare* (University of Toronto Press: Toronto, 1978).

Vickers, Brian, *The Artistry of Shakespeare's Prose* (Methuen: London, 1968).

Wells, R. H., *Shakespeare, Politics and the State* (Macmillan: Basingstoke, 1986).

Wells, Stanley (ed.), *Shakespeare: Select bibliographical guides* (Oxford University Press: London, 1973; rev. edn 1990).

Whitaker, Virgil K., *The Mirror up to Nature: The technique of Shakespeare's tragedies* (Huntington Library: San Marino, Calif., 1965).

Wilders, John, *The Lost Garden: A view of Shakespeare's English and Roman history plays* (Macmillan: London and Basingstoke, 1978).

Articles

Anderson, Peter S., 'Shakespeare's Caesar: the language of sacrifice', *CompD*, 3 (1969).

Anson, John S., 'Julius Caesar: the politics of the hardened heart', *ShS*, 2 (1966).

Auffret, Jean, 'The philosophic background of *Julius Caesar*', *CahiersE*, 5 (1974).

Ayres, H. M., 'Shakespeare's *Julius Caesar* in the light of some other versions', *PMLA*, 25 (1910).

Baines, Barbara J., 'Political and poetic revisionism in *Julius Caesar*', *The Upstart Crow*, vol. x (1990).

Barroll, J. Leeds, 'Shakespeare and Roman history', *MLR*, 53, (1958).

Barroll, J. Leeds, 'The characterisation of Octavius', *ShS*, 6 (1972 for 1970).

Barton, Anne, '*Julius Caesar* and *Coriolanus*: Shakespeare's Roman world of words', in Philip H. Highfill (ed.), *Shakespeare's Craft* (Southern Illinois University Press: Carbondale, Ill., 1982).

Barton, Anne, 'Perils of historicism', review of Stephen Greenblatt's *Learning to Curse: Essays in early modern culture*, *New York Review of Books*, 28 March 1991.

Bellringer, R. W., '*Julius Caesar*: room enough', *CRIT Q*, 12 (1970).

Bowden, William R., 'The mind of Brutus', *SQ*, 17 (1966).

Brewer, D. S., 'Brutus' crime: a footnote to *Julius Caesar*', *RES*, 3 (1952).

Burke, Kenneth, 'Antony in behalf of the play', *SoR*, I (1935): reprinted in *The Philosophy of Literary Form* (Vintage Books: New York, 1957).

Chang, J. S. M. J., '*Julius Caesar* in the light of Renaissance historiography', *JEGP*, 69 (1970).

Coursen, H. R. Jnr, 'The fall and decline of Julius Ceasar', *TSLL*, 4 (1962).

Crewe, J. V., 'Shakespeare's *Julius Caesar*', *Theoria*, 37 (1971).

Dean, Leonard, '*Julius Caesar* and modern criticism', *EJ*, 50 (1961).

Dean, Paul, 'Tudor humanism and the Roman past: a background to Shakespeare', *RenQ*, 41 (1988).

Feldman, Harold, 'Unconscious envy in Brutus', *AI*, 9 (1952).

Felheim, Marvin, 'The problem of time in *Julius Caesar*', *HLQ*, 13 (1950).

Foakes, R. A., 'An approach to *Julius Caesar*', *SQ*, 5 (1954).

Fortin, René, '*Julius Caesar*: an experiment in point of view', *SQ*, 19 (1968).

Fuzier, Jean, 'Rhetoric *versus* rhetoric: a study of Shakespeare's *Julius Caesar*, act III, scene 2', *CahiersE*, 5 (1974).

Gerenday, Lynn de, 'Play, ritualization and ambivalence in *Julius Caesar*', *L&P* (1974).

Greene, Gayle, '"The power of speech to stir men's blood": the language of tragedy in Shakespeare's *Julius Caesar*', *RenD* (n.s.), 11 (1980).

Hager, Alan, '"The teeth of emulation": failed sacrifice in *Julius Caesar*', *The Upstart Crow*, vol. viii (1988).

Hall, Vernon, Jnr, '*Julius Caesar*: a play without political bias', in Cargill Bennett and Vernon Hall Jnr (eds.), *Studies in English Renaissance Drama in Memory of Karl Julius Holzknecht* (New York University Press: New York, 1959).

Hapgood, Robert, 'Shakespeare's maimed rites: the early tragedies', *CentR*, 9 (1965).

Hapgood, Robert, '"Speak hands for me": gesture as language in *Julius Caesar*', *Drama Survey*, 5 (1966): reprinted in James L. Calderwood and Harold E. Toliver, *Essays in Shakespearean Criticism* (Prentice Hall: Englewood Cliffs, New Jersey, 1970).

Hartsock, Mildred, 'The complexity of *Julius Caesar*', *PMLA*, 81 (1966).

Henze, Richard, 'Power and spirit in *Julius Caesar*', *UR*, 36 (1970).

Herbert, Edward T., 'Myth and archetype in *Julius Caesar*', *PsyR*, 57 (1970).

Homan, S. R., 'Dion, Alexander, and Demetrius – Plutarch's forgotten *Parallel Lives* – as mirrors for Shakespeare's *Julius Caesar*', *ShS*, 8 (1975).

Houppert, Joseph W., 'Fatal logic in *Julius Caesar*', *SAB*, 39.4 (1974).

Hunter, Mark, 'Politics and character in Shakespeare's *Julius Caesar*', in *Essays by Diverse Hands, Transactions of the Royal Society of Literature* (n.s.), (1931). Also in Peter Ure (ed.), *Shakespeare's Julius Caesar*, (Casebook Series, Macmillan, London, 1969).

Kaufmann, R. J. and Clifford J. Ronan, 'Shakespeare's *Julius Caesar*: an Apollonian and comparative reading', *CompD*, 4 (1970).

Kirschbaum, Leo, 'Shakespeare's stage-blood and its critical significance', *PMLA*, 64 (1949).

Knight, W. Nicholas, 'Brutus' motivation and melancholy', *The Upstart Crow*, vol. v (Fall 1984).

Knights, L. C., 'Shakespeare and political wisdom: a note on the personalism of *Julius Caesar* and *Coriolanus*', *SR*, 61 (1953).

Levin, Richard A., 'Brutus: "Noblest Roman of them all"', *BSUF*, 23 (1982).

Levitsky, Ruth M., 'The elements were so mix'd . . .', *PMLA*, 88 (1973).

McAlindon, Thomas, 'The numbering of men and days: symbolic design in *The Tragedy of Julius Caesar*', *SP*, 81 (1984).

McNeir, Waldo F., 'Shakespeare's *Julius Caesar*: a tragedy without a *Hero*', Akademie der Wissenschaften und der Literatur in Mainz, in Kommission bei Franz Steiner, Wiesbaden (1971).

Maguin, Jean-Marc, 'Preface to a critical approach to *Julius Caesar*: Renaissance interests in Caesar; Shakespeare and North's Plutarch', *CahiersE*, 4 (1973).

Maguin, Jean-Marc, 'Play structure and dramatic technique in Shakespeare's *Julius Caesar*', *CahiersE*, 5 (1974).

Maxwell, J. C., 'Shakespeare's Roman plays: 1900–1956', *ShS*, 10 (1957).

Miola, Robert S., 'Shakespeare and his sources: observations on the critical history of *Julius Caesar*', *ShS*, 40 (1987).

Molan, Ann, '*Julius Caesar*: The general good and the singular case', *CR*, 26 (1984).

Ornstein, Robert, 'Seneca and the political drama of *Julius Caesar*', *JEGP*, 57 (1958).

Palmer, D. J., 'Tragic error in *Julius Caesar*', *SQ*, 21 (1970).

Paolucci, Anne, 'The tragic hero in *Julius Caesar*', *SQ*, 11 (1960).

Parker, Barbara L., '"This monstrous apparition": the role of perception in *Julius Caesar*', *BSUF*, 16.3 (1975).

Patrides, C. A., '"The beast with many heads": Renaissance views on the multitude', *SQ*, 16 (1965).

Payne, Michael, 'Political myth and rhetoric in *Julius Caesar*', *BuR*, 19.2 (1971).

Pechter, Edward, 'Julius Caesar and Sejanus: Roman politics, inner selves and the powers of theatre', in E. A. J. Honigmann (ed.), *Shakespeare and his Contemporaries: Essays in comparison* (Revels Plays Companion Library, Manchester University Press: Manchester, 1986).

Peterson, Douglas L., '"Wisdom consumed in confidence": an examination of Shakespeare's *Julius Caesar*', *SQ*, 16 (1965).

Pinciss, G. M., 'Rhetoric as character in the Forum speech in *Julius Caesar*', *The Upstart Crow*, vol. iv (Fall 1982).

Prior, Moody E., 'The search for a hero in *Julius Caesar*', *RenD* (n.s.), 2 (1969).

Pughe, Thomas, '"What should the wars do with these jigging fools?": the poets in Shakespeare's *Julius Caesar*', *ES*, 69 (1988).

Rackin, Phyllis, 'The pride of Shakespeare's Brutus', *LC*, 32 (1966).

Rees, Joan, '*Julius Caesar* – an earlier play, and an interpretation', *MLR*, 50 (1955).

Reynolds, Robert C., 'Ironic epithet in *Julius Caesar*', *SQ*, 24 (1973).

Ribner, Irving, 'Political issues in *Julius Caesar*', *JEGP*, 56 (1957).

Rice, Julian C., '*Julius Caesar* and the judgement of the senses', *SEL*, 13 (1973).

Sacharoff, Mark, 'Suicide and Brutus' philosophy in *Julius Caesar*', *JHI*, 33 (1972).

Sanders, Norman, 'The shift of power in *Julius Caesar*', *REL*, vol. v, no. 2 (April 1964).

Scott, William O., 'The speculative eye: problematic self-knowledge in *Julius Caesar*', *ShS*, 40 (1988).

ShS, 10 (1957) – devoted to Shakespeare's Roman plays.

ShS, 23 (1970) – issue devoted largely to style.

ShS, 31 (1979) – issue devoted to Shakespeare and the Classical World.

Smith, Warren D., 'The duplicate revelation of Portia's death', *SQ*, 4 (1953): reprinted in Julien Markels (ed.), *Shakespeare's 'Julius Caesar'* (Charles Scribner's Sons: New York, 1961).

Spakowski, R. E., 'Deification and myth-making in the play *Julius Caesar*', *UR*, 36 (1969).

Stirling, Brents, 'Brutus and the death of Portia', *SQ*, 10 (1959).

Stirling, Brents, '*Julius Caesar* in revision', *SQ*, 13 (1962).

Takada, Shigeki, 'Calls and silence – style of distance in *Julius Caesar*', *ShakS*, vol. 23 (1984–5).

Taylor, Myron, 'Shakespeare's *Julius Caesar* and the irony of history', *SQ*, 24 (1973).

Thompson, Ann, 'Does it matter which edition you use?' in Lesley Aers and Nigel Wheale (eds.), *Shakespeare in the Changing Curriculum* (Routledge: London and New York, 1991).

Toole, William B., 'The metaphor of alchemy in *Julius Caesar*', *Costerus*, 5 (1972).

Toole, William B., 'The cobbler, the disrobed image and the motif of movement in *Julius Caesar*', *The Upstart Crow*, vol. iv (Fall 1982).

Uhler, John Earle, '*Julius Caesar* – a morality of respublica', in Arthur D. Matthews and Clark M. Emery (eds.), *Studies in Shakespeare* (University of Miami Press: Coral Gables, Fla., 1953; reprinted by AMS: New York).

Vawter, Marvin L., '*Julius Caesar*: rupture in the bond', *JEGP*, 72 (1973).

Vawter, Marvin L., '"Division 'tween our souls": Shakespeare's stoic Brutus', *ShS*, 7 (1974).

Vawter, Marvin L., '"After their fashion": Cicero and Brutus in *Julius Caesar*', *SQ*, 9 (1976).

Velz, John W., 'Clemency, will and just cause in *Julius Caesar*', *ShS*, 22 (1969).

Velz, John W., 'Undular structure in *Julius Caesar*', *MLR*, 66 (1971).

Velz, John W., 'Two emblems in Brutus' orchard', *RenQ*, 25 (1972).

Velz, John W., 'Cassius as a "great observer"', *MLR*, 68 (1973).

Velz, John W., 'The ancient world in Shakespeare: authenticity or anachronism? A retrospect', *ShS*, 31 (1978).

Velz, John W., '*Orator* and *Imperator* in *Julius Caesar*: style and the process of Roman history', *ShakS*, 15 (1982).

Viswanathan, S., '"Illeism with a difference" in certain middle plays of Shakespeare', *SQ*, 20 (1969).

Walker, Roy, 'Unto Caesar: a review of recent productions', *ShS*, 11 (1958).

Welsh, Alexander, '"Brutus is an honorable man"', *YR*, 64 (1975).

Wilkinson, Andrew M., 'A psychological approach to *Julius Caesar*', *REL*, 7 (1966).

Wilson, John Dover, 'Ben Jonson and *Julius Caesar*', *ShS*, 2 (1949).

Yamada, Naomichi, 'Two tragedies in harmony in *Julius Caesar* – Shakespeare's reinterpretation of Plutarch', *Hitotsubashi Journal of Arts and Sciences*, 27 (Hitotsubashi University: Tokyo, 1986).

Yoder, R. A., 'History and the histories in *Julius Caesar*', *SQ*, 24 (1973).

Yu, Anthony C., 'O hateful error: tragic *Hamartia* in Shakespeare's Brutus', *CLAJ*, 16 (1973).

Zandvoort, R. W., 'Brutus' Forum speech in *Julius Caesar*', *RES*, 16 (1940): reprinted in R. W. Zandvoort, *Collected Papers, Groningen Studies in English*, 5 (Wolters: Groningen, 1954).

NEW APPROACHES AND RESPONSES

Books

Belsey, Catherine, *The Subject of Tragedy: Identity and difference in Renaissance drama* (Methuen: London and New York, 1985).

Bristol, Michael D., *Carnival and Theatre: Plebeian culture and the structure of authority in Renaissance England* (Methuen: New York and London, 1985).

Callaghan, Dympna, *Women and Gender in Renaissance Tragedy: A study of 'King Lear', 'Othello', 'The Duchess of Malfi', and 'The White Devil'* (Harvester Wheatsheaf: New York and London, 1989).

Dollimore, J., *Radical Tragedy: Religion, ideology and power in the drama of Shakespeare and his contemporaries* (Harvester: Brighton, 1984).

Dollimore, J. and A. Sinfield (eds.), *Political Shakespeare: New essays in cultural materialism* (Manchester University Press: Manchester, 1985).

Drakakis, J. (ed.), *Alternative Shakespeares* (Methuen: London and New York, 1985).

ELR, 16 (Winter 1986) – volume devoted to 'Studies in Renaissance Historicism'.

Goldberg, Jonathan, *James I and the Politics of Literature: Shakespeare,*

Donne, and Their Contemporaries (Johns Hopkins University Press: Baltimore, Md., 1983).

Goldman, M., *Shakespeare and the Energies of Drama* (Princeton University Press: Princeton, New Jersey, 1972).

Greenblatt, Stephen J., *Renaissance Self-Fashioning: From More to Shakespeare* (University of Chicago Press: Chicago, Ill., 1980).

Greenblatt, Stephen J., *Forms of Power and the Power of Forms in the Renaissance* (Pilgrim Books: Norman, Okl., 1982).

Greenblatt, Stephen J., *Shakespearean Negotiations: The circulation of social energy in Renaissance England* (Oxford University Press: Oxford, 1988).

Greenblatt, Stephen J., *Learning to Curse: Essays in early modern culture* (Routledge: London, 1991).

Healy, T., *New Latitudes: Theory and English Renaissance literature* (Edward Arnold: London, 1992).

Holderness, Graham (ed.), *The Shakespeare Myth* (Manchester University Press: Manchester, 1988).

Holderness, Graham, Nick Potter and John Turner, *Shakespeare: The Play of History: Contemporary interpretations of Shakespeare* (Macmillan: London, 1989).

Howard, Jean E. and Marion F. O'Connor (eds.), *Shakespeare Reproduced: The text in history and ideology* (Methuen: New York and London, 1987).

Lerner, Lawrence (ed.) *Reconstructing Literature* (Blackwell: Oxford, 1983).

Marcus, Leah S., *Puzzling Shakespeare: Local reading and its discontents* (University of California Press: Berkeley, Calif., Los Angeles and London, 1988).

Marsden, J. I. (ed.), *The Appropriation of Shakespeare* (Harvester Wheatsheaf: Hemel Hempstead, 1991).

Neely, Carol Thomas, Gayle Greene and Carolyn Ruth Swift Lenz (eds.), *The Woman's Part: Feminist criticism of Shakespeare* (University of Illinois Press: Urbana, Ill., 1980).

Parker, Patricia and Geoffrey Hartman (eds.), *Shakespeare and the Question of Theory* (Methuen: London, 1984).

Pye, C., *The Regal Phantasm: Shakespeare and the politics of spectacle* (Routledge: London, 1990).

Tennenhouse, Leonard, *Power on Display: The politics of Shakespeare's genres* (Methuen: London, 1986).

Wayne, V. (ed.), *The Matter of Difference: Materialist feminist criticism of Shakespeare* (Harvester Wheatsheaf: Hemel Hempstead, 1991).

Articles

Clare, Janet, 'Greater themes for insurrection's arguing: political censorship and the Elizabethan and Jacobean stage', *RES* (n.s.), 38 (May 1987).

Drakakis, John, '"Fashion it thus": *Julius Caesar* and the politics of theatrical representation', paper delivered at the 24th International Shakespeare Conference, Stratford-upon-Avon (August 1990); published in *ShS*, 44 (1992).

Howard, Jean, 'The new historicism in Renaissance studies', *ELR*, 16 (1986).

Levin, Richard, 'Feminist thematics and Shakespearean tragedy', *PMLA*, 103 (1988).

Levin, Richard, 'Unthinkable thoughts in the new historicizing of English Renaissance drama', *NLH*, no. 5 (Spring 1990).

McEachern, Claire, 'Fathering herself: a source study of Shakespeare's feminism', *SQ*, 39 (1988).

Neely, Carol Thomas, 'Constructing the subject: feminist practice and the new Renaissance discourses', *ELR*, 18 (1988).

Pechter, Edward, 'The new historicism and its discontents: politicizing Renaissance drama', *PMLA*, 102 (1987).

Weimann, Robert, 'Bifold authority in Shakespeare's theatre', *SQ*, 39 (1988).

White, R. S., '*King Lear* and philosophical anarchism', *ENGLISH*, vol. xxxvii, no. 159 (Autumn 1988).

Wilson, Richard, '"A mingled yarn": Shakespeare and the cloth makers', *Literature and History* (1986).

Wilson, Richard, '"Is this a holiday": Shakespeare's Roman carnival', *ELH*, 54 (1987).